19.95

BUTLER COUNTY

BUTLER COUNTY

AN ILLUSTRATED HISTORY

GEORGE C. CROUT

PICTURE RESEARCH BY ELSIE L. BATES
"PARTNERS IN PROGRESS" BY THOMAS GRANT AND
ERCEL EATON

Produced in cooperation with the
Butler County Historical Society

Windsor Publications, Inc.
Woodland Hills, California

Page two
Although this Herbert Fall painting shows the small manufacturing center at Middletown in 1802, it is typical of several other towns throughout Butler County. Most communities grew up around a sawmill, which provided lumber for building. They also had a woolen mill to process sheared wool into coarse cloth, and a grist mill which could be set to grind either corn or wheat.

Windsor Publications
History Books Division

Publisher: John M. Phillips
Production Supervisor: Katherine Cooper
Senior Picture Editor: Teri Davis Greenberg
Senior Corporate History Editor: Karen Story
Corporate History Editors: Phyllis Gray, Judith Hunter
Marketing Director: Ellen Kettenbeil
Design Director: Alexander D'Anca
Production Manager: Dee Cooper
Typesetting Manager: E. Beryl Myers
Proofreading Manager: Doris R. Malkin

Staff for *Butler County: An Illustrated History*
Editors: Kevin Cavanaugh, Teri Davis Greenberg
Production Editor: Susan Wells
Editorial Assistants: Patricia Buzard, Lonnie Le Pham, Pat Pittman
Proofreading Staff: Lynn Johnson, Jeff Leckrone
Sales Manager: Robert Moffitt
Sales Representative: Jim Koch
Layout Artist: Chris McKibbin
Production Artists: Beth Bowman, Ellen Ifrah
Typographer: Barbara Neiman

©1983 by Windsor Publications. All rights reserved.
Published 1984
Printed in the United States of America
First Edition

Library of Congress Cataloging in Publication Data

Crout, George C.
   Butler County.

   Bibliography: p.
   Includes index.
   1. Butler County (Ohio)—History. 2. Butler County (Ohio)—Description and travel. 3. Butler County (Ohio)—Industries. I. Title.
F497.B9C76   1984   977.1'75   84-5138
ISBN 0-89781-123-2

CONTENTS

Introduction 6

Acknowledgements 7

Patrons 8

Chronology 9

CHAPTER I
Butler County Beginnings 11

CHAPTER II
Fort Hamilton and Early Settlement 17

CHAPTER III
Along The Old Canal 27

CHAPTER IV
Down On The Farm 33

CHAPTER V
Business And Industry Develop 39

CHAPTER VI
Spirit, Mind, And Body: The Growth of Local Institutions 49

CHAPTER VII
Entertainment, Sports, And Recreation 63

CHAPTER VIII
Butler County: A Century Of Change 73

CHAPTER IX
Partners In Progress 95

Bibliography 123

Index 124

Introduction

On the afternoon of September 17, 1859, a tall, distinguished passenger was aboard a car on the Cincinnati, Hamilton and Dayton Railroad. After a brief stop at the Middletown Station to take on wood and water, the train proceeded to the Hamilton depot. From a platform here, Abraham Lincoln spoke for some 20 minutes to a large crowd of Butler County citizens, noting that he was in "the garden spot of the world."

Lincoln meant this literally because Butler County was one of the nation's leading agricultural producers. Hamilton, its largest and only city, had 7,000 inhabitants; Middletown had a mere 2,000. Today the county has five cities and many towns and villages.

Two major cities dominate southwestern Ohio. Cincinnati reaches up to embrace Hamilton, while Dayton's metropolitan arms stretch southward to Middletown. Between these two cities, along I-75 (the nation's highway) and bisected by the Great Miami River, is Butler County. It is a land of clear, flowing streams winding their way out of gently rolling hills on their way to the great river. In the valleys are thousands of acres of deep, fertile farmland.

In our Great Miami Valley the second major settlement in the Northwest Territory was made, even before Ohio had been born. For a brief time Hamilton was the nation's most distant settlement north and west of the Ohio River. Out of the shadows of its history emerges the frontiersman and pioneer, both of whom traveled over land once claimed by mysterious prehistoric races. Through words and pictures this book recounts the magical development of General Richard Butler's county.

Acknowledgements

An historian's work is largely that of a scribe—he collects and records what others have observed. He finds his material in dusty manuscripts, brittle newspapers, ancient courthouse basements, and precious library collections. He is a scavenger of facts and ideas of men long dead. There is no way to thank them except through a line in a bibliography.

The historian does not work alone; he is dependent on the research of his contemporaries. Butler County has many area historians. To these fellow workers, the author is greatly indebted. They include: Esther R. Benzing; Thomas F. Stander; Russell E. Huston; Jim Blount; Doris Page; Edward J. Keefe; Alice H. Hollenbaugh; Ruth J. Cast; Ophia D. Smith; Robert D. Oglesby; and Walter Havighurst. For providing access to rare local documents, thanks are extended to Butler County librarians Douglas J. Bean, Mary Pat Essman, and Irene Lindsey.

Elsie Bates served as historical photo researcher and current photographer in charge of all illustrations. She was assisted by: Weltha H. Bates; Sterling Cook; Bob Walker; Sutton G. Landry; James S. Irwin; Patrick Brown; Harold Kramer; and George Hoxie. A special note of appreciation is due Mrs. Herbert W. Fall for permission to use county sketches made by her late husband. Millicent Bender and John W. Howard also assisted with the art work, while County Engineer William R. Foster provided several maps.

The book was guided to fruition by a committee of the Butler County Historical Society composed of Elsie Bates, (chairman), Russell Huston, and George Schneidler (society board chairman). Backing the committee were the Society's officers James A. Hoerner, (president), Harold Burdsall, and Charles Stinger. Curator Helen Miller lent her talents in many ways.

PATRONS

The following individuals, companies, and organizations have made a valuable commitment to the quality of this publication. Windsor Publications and the Butler County Historical Society and Museum gratefully acknowledge their participation in *Butler County: An Illustrated History*.

Aeronca, Inc.*
Altrusa Club of Hamilton, Ohio
Armco Inc.*
The Beckett Paper Company*
Mrs. Esther R. Benzing
Black Clawson Company*
Bob's Truck Service, Inc.
Butler County Chapter of the Ohio Genealogical Society
Champion International-Hamilton
Cincinnati Bell Telephone Company
Community Federal Savings and Loan Association*
First National Bank of Southwestern Ohio*
George Anthony Gaspar, M.D.
Greenwood Cemetery Association*
Hamilton Allied Corporation*
Hamilton Caster & Mfg. Co.*
Hamilton-Fairfield Journal-News
Hamilton Industrial Grinding Inc.*
Hamilton Lumber Company
The Hamilton Tool Co.*
Mr. & Mrs. James A. Hoerner

Home Federal Savings and Loan Association*
Ina Sebald Jones
Edward J. Keefe
The Las-Stik Manufacturing Company*
LEAP & Associates, REALTORS
Liberty Township Historical Society
Mercy Hospital*
Middletown Federal Savings & Loan Association
Middletown Historical Society
Mrs. Helen L. Miller
Mosler An American-Standard Company*
Mr. & Mrs. Richard L. Nevel
Louise & Robert Dickey Oglesby
Mr. & Mrs. George A. Schneidler
Virgil Schwarm Investment Securities
Martha L. and Robert E. Scudder
Second National Bank of Hamilton*
Society Bank
Solar America Inc./Challenger Corp.
James A. Stewart, M.D.
Trenton Historical Society
(in memory of) Wilfred D. Vorhis
Woodside Cemetery*
WPFB Radio Station

*Partners in Progress of *Butler County: An Illustrated History*. The histories of these companies and organizations appear in Chapter 9, beginning on page 95.

CHRONOLOGY

1791 Clarkson Freeman bought 630 acres on the site later occupied by Lesourdsville
1795 Celadon Symmes settled in Fairfield Township area
1797 First cabin built in the Blue Ball area
1800 Huntsville founded
1802 Middletown laid out; Hamilton platted; and the first settler arrived in the Collinsville area
1803 Shandon laid out (originally Paddy's Run, New London, and Glendower)
1804 Fairfield Township created by the Ohio legislature; Hamilton's post office opened
1810 Jeptha Garrigus built first grist mill at Black Bottom
1812 Clawson's Post Office established (later Princeton); Pisgah platted
1814 Darrtown laid out
1816 Princeton post office opened; Trenton platted; Jacksonburg platted; and Miltonville laid out
1817 Huntsville post office opened; Ross platted; and Mechanicsburgh platted (formerly Hogtown)
1818 West Liberty platted (later Poasttown)
1820 Blumfield became Trenton
1823 Scipio's post office opened
1824 Somerville post office opened; Mechanicsburgh became Chester (later West Chester)
1825 Reily post office opened
1827 Hamilton incorporated
1830 College Corner platted
1831 Somerville platted
1833 Middletown incorporated
1835 Hart's Block platted
1839 First brick house in Bethany built
1840 Astoria post office opened
1841 Seven Mile platted
1842 Tylersville platted (originally Pug Muncy)
1844 Huntsville post office moved to Bethany
1848 Reily platted (10/25); and West Liberty became Poasttown
1850 Flenner's Corner platted
1852 McGonigle School built; Bunker Hill post office opened
1853 Okena platted
1854 Hamilton became a city
1855 Jones Station platted (later Stockton); Benjamin Le Sourd sold land to A.H. Knoor Company for ice cutting ponds
1858 Wood's Station built
1867 Woodsdale laid out
1882 Heno post office opened (4/18)
1886 Middletown became a city
1900 Armco, Inc. opened in Middletown
1901 New Miami coke plant opened
1909 Williamsdale platted
1920 Ford tractor plant opened in Hamilton
1921 Edgar Streifthau bought Knoor ice ponds and built Le Sourdsville Lake (now called Americana)
1928 Oneida platted by Crist Realty Company
1945 General Motors plant opened in Fairfield Township
1953 Fairfield Civic Association founded (10/28)
1954 Fairfield incorporated (7/10)
1955 Fairfield becomes Butler County's third largest city
1958 Middletown receives the All-America City Award from the National Municipal League
1962 Fairfield post office opened
1971 Trenton became a city

CHAPTER I
Butler County Beginnings

France once claimed the area of Butler County as part of the Province of Quebec. After planting a leaden plate marker at the river's mouth, Captain Céléron de Bienville ascended the Great Miami with a large expedition of more than 200 men to strengthen and confirm France's ownership.

Butler County lies in southwestern Ohio between Hamilton and Montgomery Counties, sharing the northern boundary with Preble County. To the east is Warren County; to the west is the Indiana state line.

Butler County ranks third in population among the 14 counties that comprise the Miami Valley, being situated between the valley's two most populous counties. The three counties—Hamilton, Montgomery, and Butler—account for over one half the population of the Miami Valley. The 1980 census lists Butler with a population of 258,787, as tenth in population among Ohio's 88 counties.

THE LANDSCAPE TAKES SHAPE Geologists have discovered fossilized remains of sea animals imbedded in limestone that indicate that Butler County was once part of an island that rose from an ancient sea. Thousands of years ago rivers began to form. The oldest of these is known as the Teays, which rose in the Southern Appalachians, eventually reaching West Central Ohio on the way north. Its tributaries thus drained northward. The first such stream, known as the Hamilton River, was a creation of the Kansas Glacier. In a later geological period a new Middletown River was formed by glacial action that reversed the old drainage pattern, moving it southward, and forming the Ohio River. The work of the Middletown River was taken over by what became the Great Miami.

Glaciers changed the face of the land. The Illinoian Glacier created the Middletown River. This glacier's work can still be seen on the smoothed, striated rock surfaces on the bluff south of Excello through which Route 4 was cut. The Wisconsin Glacier, and last glacier to change the land of Butler County, crept down over the area between 10,000 and 20,000 years ago. The Wisconsin Glacier, which may have reached a thickness of 300 feet, reversed rivers, deposited boulders, dropped tons of drift and till, deposited moraines, dug out ponds, and created new river channels. It made the path for the present Great Miami River and its tributaries. The glacier left a variety of rich soils in the Miami Valley, especially in Butler County. This soil, plus a moderate climate with adequate rainfall, makes a land rich in agricultural wealth.

The Great Miami River flows into the Ohio just west of Cincinnati where it receives the waters of the Whitewater River of Indiana. Cutting diagonally through Butler County, the river flows south from Middletown through Hamilton and past Fairfield and Ross townships to the southern county line. In South Middletown the floodplain of the Great Miami broadens, providing the sites for Excello, Amanda, and Trenton.

BUTLER COUNTY

The valley reaches its widest point of 2.5 miles just northeast of Hamilton at Hickory Flats, long considered one of the most fertile farming areas in Ohio.

Both the location of Hamilton and Middletown were determined by the Great Miami River. In pioneer days the river was a highway of commerce with its waters feeding the Miami Canal system. Its floodplain served as a natural path on which roads were built and railroads constructed. The wide floodplain at both cities provided good level building land for industrial and residential development.

THE FIRST INHABITANTS The first people to come to Ohio were nomads who lived by hunting. No one knows exactly when the earliest people arrived in the region, but it was many thousands of years ago. Scientists believe they migrated from Siberia in northern Asia and crossed the Bering Strait during the Ice Age when an ice bridge formed between the two continents. One group moved southward, and some migrants stopped in the Miami Valley. Although the prehistoric people who lived in Butler County before written history are often known as the Mound Builders, they represent several groups of ancient people: the Archaic, Adena, Hopewell, and Fort Ancient.

First to appear were the Archaic people. They settled along the rivers of the county, using the streams for water and fishing. They were so dependent on the water that archeologists often call them the river people. They ate shelled water animals, such as mollusks. Found in cooking ashes were charred bones of turkeys, foxes, rabbits, squirrels, water fowl, hulls of acorns, nuts, and roots. Around the ashes were found such artifacts as stone hammers, stone axes, and even pestles for grinding grain. Circular graves have been discovered. The discovery of post holes, found in patterns, indicates that the Archaic people probably erected shelters by stretching skins over posts. The Adena people who lived in Butler County before 800 B.C., developed a more advanced culture than that of the Archaic people.

Though still hunters, the Adena people learned to farm. They grew pumpkins, squash, beans, corn, and sunflowers. They lived in round dwellings, each with a smoke hole in the center. Houses were grouped in villages and each one had a common meeting place. The Adena people also knew how to weave and dye cloth. They built cradle boards, made smoking pipes, and developed a monotheistic system of religion.

The Adena people created striking earthworks. The Great Mound of Butler County is the highest in the county. It is located west of Middletown on the Wayne-Madison Road atop a high hill on what was once the old Long farm. From the mound's top, a person can enjoy a 20-mile view of the region.

With the decline of the Adena culture, another civilization developed in the county. The Hopewell people built mounds, many of which were used largely for burial. Their highest mounds served as signal mounds,

Right
This medicine man, or shaman, was a member of the Miami Indian tribe. The Indians thought he had supernatural powers of a religious nature, and was in contact with the Great Spirit. Tribesmen consulted him on medical problems using his knowledge of herbs and drugs with curative powers. His costume was elaborate, each item involving symbolism.

Far right
The Great Butler Mound commands more than a 20-mile view of the valley. As shown in this painting by artist Herbert Fall, Indian watchmen could send smoke signals to warn fellow tribesmen of danger. Both the Kinder Mound at Franklin and the Miamisburg Mound, the largest Adena mound in the state, were within range. Courtesy, Middletown Historical Society

BUTLER COUNTY BEGINNINGS

BUTLER COUNTY

Not only did the Hopewell people produce beautiful clay smoking pipes, but they achieved a very high artistic level with their pottery. Tempering their ware with crushed, granitic stone, the Hopewells made colors for their pieces ranging from gray to buff.

while mound enclosures were built for defense.

The greatest monument of the Hopewell people is in neighboring Warren County. It is known as Fort Ancient. This last great Mound Builder civilization merged into the last of the prehistoric cultures, known as the Fort Ancient peoples. They took over the old Hopewell sites, adapting them to meet their needs.

THE INDIANS Although recent research has uncovered an ancient Indian tribe known as the Mosopelea, the first Indians encountered by white men in the valley were the Miamis. The Miami Indians were first reported by French missionaries along the Fox River in Wisconsin around 1670. After being driven out of that area the Miamis were found along the St. Joseph River in Illinois. By 1711 they were in the Wabash River Valley of northeastern Indiana. Other tribes moved in, forcing the Miami Indians to move southward. They finally settled along both the Miami and the Maumee. The Miamis had a large settlement near present-day Fort Wayne, but their main town became Pickawillany, near what is now Piqua. Chief Little Turtle was their most famous chief.

The Miamis eventually migrated north, and white settlers moved into the Miami Valley and occupied the old Indian lands. The early pioneers of the county found two fertile areas, the Little Prairie at Middletown and the Great Prairie between Middletown and Hamilton.

The Shawnee Indians' homeland was in what became the Carolinas, Tennessee, Kentucky, and in Ohio their settlements were found in the valley of the Scioto. Then they pushed over into the valley of the Little Miami, and finally into the Great Miami River Valley. So when the white settlers arrived, they fought the Shawnee, who were much more hostile than the Miamis. Perhaps the Shawnee better understood the meaning of the white settlement, for at one time they had lived along the seacoast and had been driven westward across the Appalachians by the colonists.

Finally the Miami Indians realized that their homes in northern Ohio and Indiana would also be lost, so they joined the Shawnee and other tribes in a confederation to save their homelands. From the viewpoint of the white pioneer, the Ohio lands were considered unoccupied; he thought he had the right to settle and use these lands. The rich soil could support many people. The Indians and the white man both resorted to force. The savage violence on both sides lead to a military campaign against the Indians by the new national government headed by President George Washington. In ensuing years a guerrilla war was fought between the Indians and the settlers. In 1785 near the mouth of the Great Miami River, Fort Finney was erected. General George Rogers Clark, S.H. Parsons, and General Richard Butler, who was to give his name to the county, were asked by the new federal government to meet with the Indians. At that time General Butler was the Indian Commissioner for this district. The Shawnee arrived in January 1786. General Clark finally offered the Shawnee peace. The Indians agreed to the Treaty of Fort Finney, which drew the line between them and the white settlers at a point just south of the present-day site of Piqua. Thus southern Ohio, which was to include Butler County, was officially removed from Indian control.

THE FIRST WHITE SETTLERS ARRIVE In 1785 the first white settlers had arrived in Butler County. John Hindman left Pennsylvania in March 1785 for the Northwest Territory. In the Hindman party were William West, John Simmons, John Sept, and a Mr. Carlin, along with their families. Starting at the mouth of Buffalo Creek, they floated down the Ohio River to Limestone, now Maysville, Kentucky. Here they stopped to rest for two weeks.

Their next stop was at the mouth of the Great Miami River. This was the first group of white settlers to have landed there, and Fort Finney had not yet been constructed. While the party was camped there, the Ohio River rose to flood stage and the lowlands along the Big Miami were covered. The party crossed to the Kentucky side where they stayed a few months. With the waters down, the party started up the Great Miami. They came to the mouth of the Whitewater River and thinking it to be the main channel they proceeded up that river. But Joseph Robinson, who had joined the group at the mouth of the Great Miami, soon realized that they were on the wrong river. Since he knew the country, the party returned to the point where the rivers met and ascended the Great Miami.

The Hindman party continued up the river to the place where the floodplain widened to about two miles. This site later became the city of Hamilton. Here was the best bottom land the frontiersmen had ever seen. They selected choice farming lands and proceeded to mark off their claims.

Of course, the Hindman group was not the only party of frontiersmen who had rushed in to make claims to land in southern Ohio during and following the American Revolution. An estimated 1,500 other people came to settle in the region during that period.

CHAPTER II
Fort Hamilton And Early Settlement

Early Butler County residents often observed Indians across the Miami River. Two Indian hunters are depicted here returning to their homes at the site now marked by the west end of the bridge at Trenton.

THE SYMMES PURCHASE In 1787 Judge John Cleves Symmes and a party set out to explore the Miami Valley. On August 29, 1787, Judge Symmes submitted a proposal to Congress to purchase all the land lying between the two Miami rivers at one dollar an acre. Unable to raise enough money for the million acres he wanted, Symmes had to be satisfied with 311,682 acres.

Before receiving his government contract, Symmes sent out an advance party headed by Major Benjamin Stites. This party arrived at Pittsburgh and floated down the Ohio River, landing on November 18, 1788, about a mile below the mouth of the Little Miami River. Here the party set up a village named Columbia, the first settlement in the Miami Valley.

On December 28, the Matthias Denman party that had purchased 1,000 acres from Symmes, anchored at Yeatman's Cove. The following day they began to build the first log cabin on the site that was to become Cincinnati. It was not until February 2, 1789, that Judge Symmes and his party landed at North Bend, east of the mouth of the Great Miami.

Judge Symmes hired 13 surveyors to lay out the land and set up the townships. The northern boundary of the tract was just north of what is now Todhunter Road at Monroe. This left the northern part of Butler County, including Middletown, out of his control. The land west of the river remained the property of the U.S. government. These lands were put up for sale in 1800. Judge Symmes' survey of the land and a boundary misunderstanding led to many legal battles in the early courts. The judge himself, however, was highly respected as the man who planned the first settlement in the Miami Valley.

BUILDING THE FORT Hunting and exploration parties traveled up the Miami Valley, seeking choice farm land. Some obtained title to these lands but remained in the Cincinnati area under the protection of Fort Washington, erected in 1789. Even though negotiation with the Indians had been made for the land, hostility continued. Small groups of pioneers north of Cincinnati erected blockhouses where they could gather in case of attack.

President Washington decided to use military force against the Indians. Congress gave the President authority to call up the militia of Kentucky, Virginia, and Pennsylvania with orders to meet at Fort Washington. The expedition was organized with 1,450 men, only 330 of whom were regular army, under the command of General Josiah Harmar. The army moved northward along the Little Miami River, crossed over to the Great

The construction of Fort Washington began in September 1789, approximately 10 months after the first settlement at Cincinnati. The fort provided security for the settlers and served as a base of operations for the campaign against the Indians in western Ohio.

Miami, and marched on the Indian towns. Little Turtle, with a strong force, ambushed a part of the expedition, inflicting heavy casualties— 183 killed, 35 wounded. Harmar returned to Fort Washington in disgrace. President Washington appointed General Arthur St. Clair to replace Harmar on March 4, 1791.

St. Clair understood that a chain of forts needed to be built. These forts would stretch north from Fort Washington to the Maumee Valley, where the Indians had a stronghold. Each fort was to be a day's march apart. The first one to be constructed was Fort Hamilton.

On September 17, 1791, St. Clair ordered Colonel William Darke and his men to the bend of the Great Miami River at what was to become the site of Fort Hamilton. St. Clair followed Darke to the site within a few days. He selected the location for the fort, marked off the area, and construction began. St. Clair noted that the site would command control of the river, offer a good place for storage of supplies, and form the first link in his proposed chain of forts. Fort Hamilton was named after Alexander Hamilton, who was Secretary of the Treasury at the time.

The fort was a stockade with a perimeter of about 1,000 feet. Sturdy log pickets set in a three-foot deep trench enclosed the fort. Four blockhouses were erected, two with cannon; one cannon faced the higher land, and the other faced the river ford. Barracks were built for the officers and men. The magazine, where ammunition was stored, was a large sturdy building with a hipped roof. The officers' mess was a frame building that later served as Butler County's first courthouse. By September 30, 1791, the fort was largely completed, and with its two pieces of artillery in place, a salute was fired and the fort officially named.

INDIAN WARFARE Just three days before the fort's dedication, General Richard Butler, second in command under General St. Clair, arrived at the fort. Butler's late arrival was due to his recruitment of troops in Pennsylvania. Now, with the troops at Fort Hamilton, he made a final inspection.

St. Clair instructed the officers on the plan of campaign. On October 3, he returned to Fort Washington to pick up another company of militia that had marched in late from Kentucky. St. Clair ordered Butler to march out of Fort Hamilton the next morning. The troops crossed the Great Miami at the ford and marched to a creek, which they named Two Mile, due to the distance marched. Four Mile and Seven Mile creeks were similarly named. By October 13, the expedition had travelled 44 miles north of Fort Hamilton.

Butler suggested that because of the lateness of the season and the condition of some of his men, that St. Clair select the thousand best trained troops and make a rapid march to the Maumee River to set up a fortification. St. Clair rejected the proposal and ordered all to march northward. By the evening of November 3, 1791, the troops had reached the southeastern fork of the Wabash River at the site where General Anthony Wayne later built Fort Recovery. The troops were on high ground, but they were too crowded to take advantage of the site. The militia camped across the stream a short distance to the north.

At sunrise 1,500 Indians attacked the American camp. The poorly trained Americans rushed to the center of the camp and chaos ensued. The Americans tried to shoot back, but most of the warriors were hidden behind trees. St. Clair tried to reorganize his men as the Indians shot four horses from under him.

St. Clair ordered a retreat. The Indians concentrated on scouring the battleground for guns and other supplies, so many soldiers escaped. In all, 593 soldiers and 37 officers were killed including General Richard Butler. Nearly 300 men returned to Fort Jefferson wounded. It was the worst defeat the U.S. Army ever suffered at the hands of the Indians, even greater than Custer's loss at Little Bighorn.

General Anthony Wayne replaced St. Clair and used Fort Hamilton as a supply post for the line of forts that he had constructed above Fort Jefferson. He built Fort Greenville and Fort Recovery, the latter on the site of St. Clair's disastrous defeat. At the junction of the Maumee and Auglaize rivers he erected Fort Defiance, the name indicating his attitude toward the Indians.

North of Fort Defiance was a forest through which a tornado had passed. The Indians grouped in this area of fallen timbers for safety and defense. The Americans, under Wayne, met the enemy on August 20, 1794. This time the Americans were ready, and in a few hours had defeated the Indian warriors. Only 35 soldiers were killed and 101 wounded. The Indian casualties were twice that number. Ten of the 19 Indian chiefs on the field had been killed. The victory at the Battle of Fallen Timbers was decisive.

General Wayne asked the Indian leaders to meet at Greenville, where on August 3, 1795, they signed the Treaty of Greenville. Wayne ordered Fort Hamilton vacated in the fall of 1795. The public property was sold at auction, and the fort was abandoned.

SETTLING AND DIVIDING THE LAND The Treaty of Greenville opened the way for immigration. Many settlers had read of the rich Miami Valley, and Judge Symmes had publicized his lands through handbills. The fertile soil produced 100 bushels of corn per acre, while 10 to 12 bushels was a common yield in the East. Jobs awaited people of all trades.

The years between 1795 and 1825 were the days of the pioneer in Butler County. The farm family, which represented over 90 percent of the population, raised crops to provide food for themselves, and to sell for cash or to barter for necessary items. Farmers often lived in isolation, with neighbors living far away. People came together to form local governments to perform tasks that families could not do alone, such as building and maintaining roads and establishing schools.

In 1794 one of the area's most competent surveyors, Israel Ludlow, laid

John Cleves Symmes was born on Long Island, New York, in 1742. A teacher and surveyor, he became a colonel in the American Revolution, and served as a judge in the Northwest Territory in 1787.

General Arthur St. Clair, Revolutionary War hero and first governor of the Northwest Territory, was born in Scotland in 1734. Gaining combat experience during the French and Indian War, he became a general during the American Revolution. He was a member of the Continental Congress before coming to Ohio in 1789.

General Anthony Wayne was a brilliant general of the Revolutionary War, serving under George Washington. Due to his recklessness and bravery, he earned the nickname "Mad Anthony." Wayne conquered the Ohio Indian Confederacy, and presided at the signing of the Treaty of Greenville in 1795.

out a town around Fort Hamilton called Fairfield. He purchased the land in 1795. Some of the soldiers at the fort stayed on as settlers. The town eventually took its name from the fort, and the city of Fairfield was later located at another site. Daniel Doty, who had marked a site along the Great Miami in 1791, returned to New Jersey in 1795 for his family. In 1796 he built his cabin on the spot he had selected. In 1802 Stephen Vail laid out the village of Middletown.

From Lexington, Massachusetts, came John Hancock, a relative of the man of the same name who had signed the Declaration of Independence. In 1798 this John Hancock built his cabin in a thick forest at the point where Main and High streets cross in Oxford today. He extended his holdings and by 1812 owned 1,600 acres between Oxford and McGonigle. Samuel McCullough built his cabin and tavern on Lot Number One on what is now South Campus Avenue in Oxford.

Edward Bebb of Wales built a house on Dry Fork near Paddy's Run, which is now called Shandon. Here William Bebb was born on December 8, 1802. He was the first native-born Ohioan to become governor of the state.

Another early family on Paddy's Run was John Halstead, whose grandson, Murat Halstead, became a noted editor of a Cincinnati newspaper. This area was Ohio's first Welsh settlement.

In 1800 the U.S. government sold the lands west of the Great Miami River that were not part of the Symmes Purchase. In that year Henry Rhea purchased 1,847 acres. Matthew Heuston, who was with Wayne during the Indian campaigns, purchased land along Four Mile Creek. Captain Samuel W. Beeler bought a section in Oxford Township at the foot of Chaw Raw Hill. In 1806 he sold some of his land to son-in-law Joel Collins, an Indian scout and fighter, who erected a powder mill on Collin's Run.

On the Great Miami's west bank, Michael Pearce of Essex County, New Jersey, purchased about 1,500 acres of land in 1801. Here, in the same year, he built a three-story brick house at what became Number One South Miami Street. In 1815 Pearce and David Enyart laid out a town called Blumfield which eventually became Trenton.

In 1800 John Baker settled on a farm on high ground south of Dicks Creek. He sold the land to Nathaniel Sackett and a partner, John H. Platt. These two platted a village in 1817 which they named in honor of the President, James Monroe.

The population of Butler County in 1810 is listed as 11,150 on the census records. Most of the people, however, lived on farms. Hamilton had fewer than 75 buildings.

Butler County's official birthday is March 24, 1803. Ohio was created March 1, 1803, making it the 17th state. The Ohio General Assembly passed an act to divide Hamilton and Ross counties, an act in which they created Butler and other counties. By 1815 Butler County's boundaries

Arthur St. Clair designed Fort Hamilton after Fort Ligonier, near his Pennsylvania home. After serving its purpose, Fort Hamilton was abandoned in 1796, but some of its buildings remained until about 1812.

BUTLER COUNTY

The most famous war chief of the Shawnee tribe, Blue Jacket, was not really an Indian. Marmaduke Van Swearingen was captured by the Shawnees when he was 17, was adopted into their tribe, and rose to the rank of chief. After his defeat at Fallen Timbers, he signed the Treaty of Greenville, and lived in Canada until his death in 1810. This portrait was painted by one of his descendants, Olive Swearingen Randall. Courtesy, Butler County Historical Society

were fixed.

On April 15, 1803, the Ohio legislature appointed James Silvers, Benjamin Stites, and David Sutton to select the best site for the county seat of justice. They met in July 1803 and proceeded on their assignment. Several towns wanted to be the county seat, for such a designation would add to the importance and growth of the locale and enrich landowners there. One site examined was along the west bank of the Great Miami River about four miles north of Hamilton. Known as High Bank, it was owned by Wilson McClellan and George Torrance. Another site considered was a large tract along the west side of the river opposite the town of Hamilton, which became Rossville. Even Middletown was in the running because Stephen Vail, when he platted the village, had reserved a site for the courthouse. Of course, this was before the county lines had been drawn. Many expected that the new county would include land farther to the north of Hamilton County than it did.

Israel Ludlow, who platted Hamilton, submitted a proposal to the commissioners. It read:

I will give for the use of the county a square for public buildings, agreeably to the plan recorded of the town of Hamilton... in case the honorable commissioners should conceive the town of Hamilton as a convenient and suitable place of justice; and will also pay two hundred dollars toward the erection of the court-house.

The commissioner chose this offer, as Hamilton, situated near the center of the new county, was the best location for the county seat. The judges, appointed by the Ohio legislature on May 10, 1803, held the first court session in the tavern owned by John Torrence at the corner of Dayton and Water streets. The tavern was in Torrence's home, the first frame building erected in Hamilton outside the fort.

At the first session the judges, James Dunn, John Greer, and John Kitchel, appointed John Reily their clerk. The first order of business for the judges was the division of the county into five townships. The judges then ordered that a trustees election be held in the townships on June 1, 1803. A county-wide election was also held for a sheriff and coroner to serve until the general election in October.

In 1804 the Ohio General Assembly passed a law that gave the county commissioners the authority to alter the township boundaries or to establish new townships. The original townships were Fairfield, Liberty, Lemon, St. Clair, and Ross. Between 1804 and 1823, the county commissioners created eight new townships. Wayne, Milford, and Reily townships were cut out of St. Clair. Milford was then subdivided, creating Oxford Township. Out of Ross Township came Morgan Township. Hanover Township was carved from Reily and St. Clair. Madison Township was separated from Lemon. In 1823 Union Township was created

FORT HAMILTON AND EARLY SETTLEMENT

Left
When this view of Hamilton and Rossville was sketched in 1840, Hamilton's population was 1,409. The same year Hamilton had seven churches, two newspapers, 13 industrial enterprises, and 16 mercantile stores. The covered bridge had been erected in 1817 by Nathan and Ira Hunt of Huntsville.

Far left
Jane Potter Sutphin, daughter of Moses and Rhoda Potter, was born April 2, 1797, the first girl to be born in the northern part of Butler County. Her mother was reportedly the first white woman to live north of Fort Hamilton.

from Liberty.

The plat of Hamilton was officially recorded on April 28, 1802, at Cincinnati because it was then in Hamilton County. Hamilton's first unofficial plat, however, was drawn on December 17, 1794, by Israel Ludlow, who had named the town Fairfield. While the state historical society usually bases the date of the founding of a town upon the official registration of its plat, a town built on the site of a fort, may use the date of the fort's completion as its founding date. Thus, Hamilton can claim 1791. Among the first settlers in Hamilton were: Darius Orcut, John Green, William McClelland, John Sutherland, John Torrence, Benjamin Randolph, Benjamin Davis, Isaac Wiles, Andrew Christy, and William Hubbert.

In 1802 Stephen Vail drew up the official plat of the Middletown with the help of James Sutton. Among the first settlers in Middletown were: Daniel Doty, Enos and Moses Potter, Calvin Morrell, James Brady, Cyrus Osbourn, Elisha Wade, Richard Watts, Abner Enoch, Garrett Vanness, Stephen Vail, and his sons Aaron and Shobal.

In April 1801 some of the public lands on the west side of the river were sold at auction. At Hamilton a company composed of Jacob Burnet, James Smith, William Ruffin, John Sutherland, and Henry Brown purchased a parcel of land. Here they platted the town of Rossville. It was not until 1854 that Hamilton and Rossville were united.

As predicted the choice of Hamilton as the county seat gave impetus to that town's growth. In 1804 it was awarded a post office by President Thomas Jefferson. John Reily was appointed as the first postmaster of what was then the United States' westernmost post office north of the Ohio River. In 1803 Hamilton planned its first county building, a jail, with construction made possible by a subscription drive. The first tax duplicate in 1804 listed 58 lots in Hamilton. By 1810 a census revealed 210 people living there, with 84 in Rossville, and 186 in Middletown.

CHAPTER III
Along The Old Canal

The canal and its spillways provided excellent fishing spots, as these anglers attest. The fish caught were prized, and provided food for the fishermen's tables. This photograph was taken at Doty's Grove sometime in the 1890s. Courtesy, Middletown Historical Society

BUILDING THE CANAL The Great Miami River provided the first artery of commerce for the valley, but, as business and industry developed, a better means of transportation was needed. The Miami Canal was begun in 1825 to meet such a need. Starting north of Middletown, the canal followed the valley of the Great Miami southward to Hamilton, where it veered to the southeast across the swampy plains to the Millcreek Valley, down through Lockland and Carthage, and into the heart of Cincinnati.

The canal was part of a federal transportation improvement program. New York had built the Erie Canal, and the two Ohio canals with ports on Lake Erie would feed into that canal and enhance trade with New York City by tying the Ohio country to the East, rather than to New Orleans. The grand plan was adopted by Ohio legislature. In 1822 the legislature appropriated money for a survey, which lead to the building of the canal.

The first spadeful of dirt for the canal was dug from the rich earth of the Daniel Doty farm at Middletown. On July 21, 1825, Governor Clinton of New York and Governor Morrow of Ohio presided over the groundbreaking ceremony, with each governor, and future President William Henry Harrison, lifting a piece of sod.

The small village of Middletown recognized the significance of the canal. Such citizens as Daniel Doty, Abner Enoch, Hugh Vail, John Sutphen, John Martin, Arthur Lefferson, and Peter Vanderveer worked hard to see that the canal passed through Middletown. Starting at Middletown, the canal was built in two directions: north to Dayton and south to Cincinnati. At that time it was the Miami Canal; later it would be extended to Toledo and become the Miami-Erie Canal. Eventually the canal cost over eight million dollars, using state funds and federal subsidies.

Each section of the canal was let for bids, so several contractors were building at the same time. About 1,000 men worked between Middletown and Cincinnati. It was the first time that many rural workers had been paid in currency. When the Irish heard of the jobs created, they flocked to the Miami Valley to help dig the canal. On July 1, 1827, the first water was let into the Miami Canal.

TRANSPORTATION AND ENERGY A Middletown craftsman, Robert L. Campbell, built the first boat used on the canal, the *Samuel Forrer* (named in honor of the canal's divisional engineer). His boat made short trips on the canal as early as July 4th at Middletown, but it was not until

November 1827 that the *Samuel Forrer* reached Hamilton, where it took many Hamiltonians on short rides. By November 1828 the way was clear from Middletown to Cincinnati, and in January 1829 the *Governor Brown* made the first trip between Cincinnati and Dayton. By 1832 it was estimated that over 1,000 people a week were passing through Butler County on the canal.

Fleets of canal boats once traveled the waters of the Miami-Erie Canal, bringing in supplies and carrying Butler County products to outside markets. A freight, or line, boat, designed to carry produce and manufactured goods, had a capacity of 60 tons. The packet boats carried passengers and served as excursion boats. Woodsdale Island attracted picnickers for a day's outing. Maintenance boats, operated by the state government, patrolled the canal, watching for burrowing animals that could break down the banks, and making necessary repairs. A typical canal boat was 60 to 75 feet long and about 14 feet wide.

While horses and mules were both used to pull boats, it was the mules that proved the cheapest and most durable on the towpath. The animals were used in pairs, and the number of pairs depended on the load. Some of the lines had way stations along the canal where horse or mule teams were changed, while others kept a spare pair of animals on the boat itself. In order to prevent wave erosion, canal boats were pulled at about four miles per hour.

The Miami-Erie Canal served other needs. At the locks the excess water could be diverted into a race, providing power to turn a waterwheel. Daniel's Mill at Hamilton and similar mills were found at many locks. The race took the water from above the lock and guided it to turn great wooden wheels. The water returned to the canal below the lock. Water from the canal was also drawn off into shallow lakes, and in the winter ice was cut and stored in great warehouses to be sold in the summer.

THE CANAL ERA ENDS The canal passed through the center of Middletown, but it only skirted eastern Hamilton. A lateral cut called the Basin brought the canal downtown. It wound eastward using the Pennsylvania right-of-way to Fourth Street at Court. Lined with wharves and warehouses, the Basin was about 200 feet wide and three-fifths of a mile long. It was filled in 1877.

The canal lasted another quarter of a century, but Hamilton shipments were made from warehouses and wharves at High Street. When the railroad came to Butler County in 1851, canal traffic began to decline. By 1860 it was losing commerce, even though the canal was still cheaper for shipping bulky materials. The passenger trade dried up entirely, except for excursion pleasure rides.

Many area citizens refused to let the canal die; they continued to believe in its future. While admitting the hardworking mule was too slow, they evolved a plan to use electric power. In 1900 the Miami and Erie Transportation Company was formed. The company stretched a trolley wire

Right
Between 1826 and 1860 the canal was the main transportation means in the county. Freight boats such as the *Black Hawk* carried cargo, packet boats transported passengers, and line boats carried both. After 1860 the passenger trade was taken over by the faster-moving railroad. Courtesy, Middletown Historical Society

Far right
The Miami-Erie Canal stretched from Cincinnati on the Ohio River north to Toledo on Lake Erie. The canal measured 40 feet wide at the top, 26 feet at the bottom, and four feet deep. The towpath averaged 10 feet wide and had a berm of about five feet. Courtesy, Carillon Park, Dayton, Ohio

TRANSPORTATION.

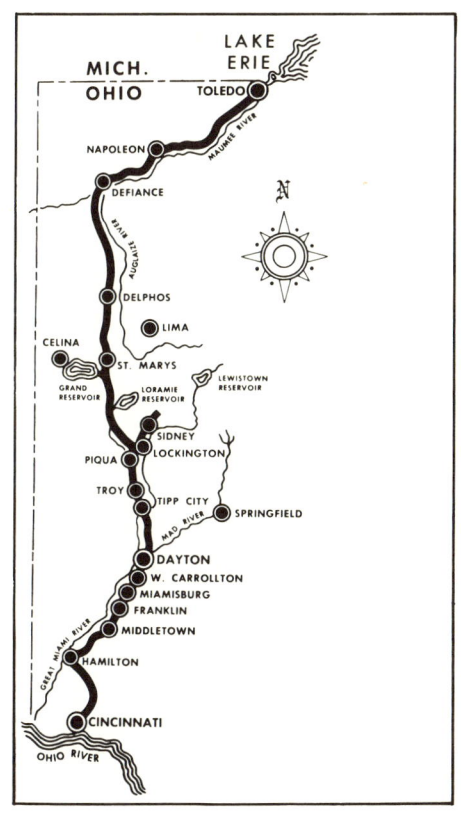

THE subscriber is still engaged in the business of running the good canal boat BLACK HAWK, and for the better accommodation of his customers, will leave Middletown every Tuesday morning, and Cincinnati every Thursday evening or Friday morning, and carry freight on the following terms, viz:

Whisky,	26	cents per barrel.	
Pork,	29	" "	"
Flour,	18	" "	"
Merchandise,	18	" "	100 lbs.
Iron, Nails and Castings,	15	" "	"
Salt,	25	" "	"
Lumber,	$2 00	" "	M feet.
Shingles,	25	" "	M
Lath,	37	" "	M
Cut Stone,	12	" "	100 lbs.
Corn,	5	" "	bushel.
Oats and Barley,	4	" "	"
Wheat,	6	" "	"

and other freight in the same proportion. The above prices include the commission for selling and making return of the money.

Dec 7 20—w   WM. McADAMS.

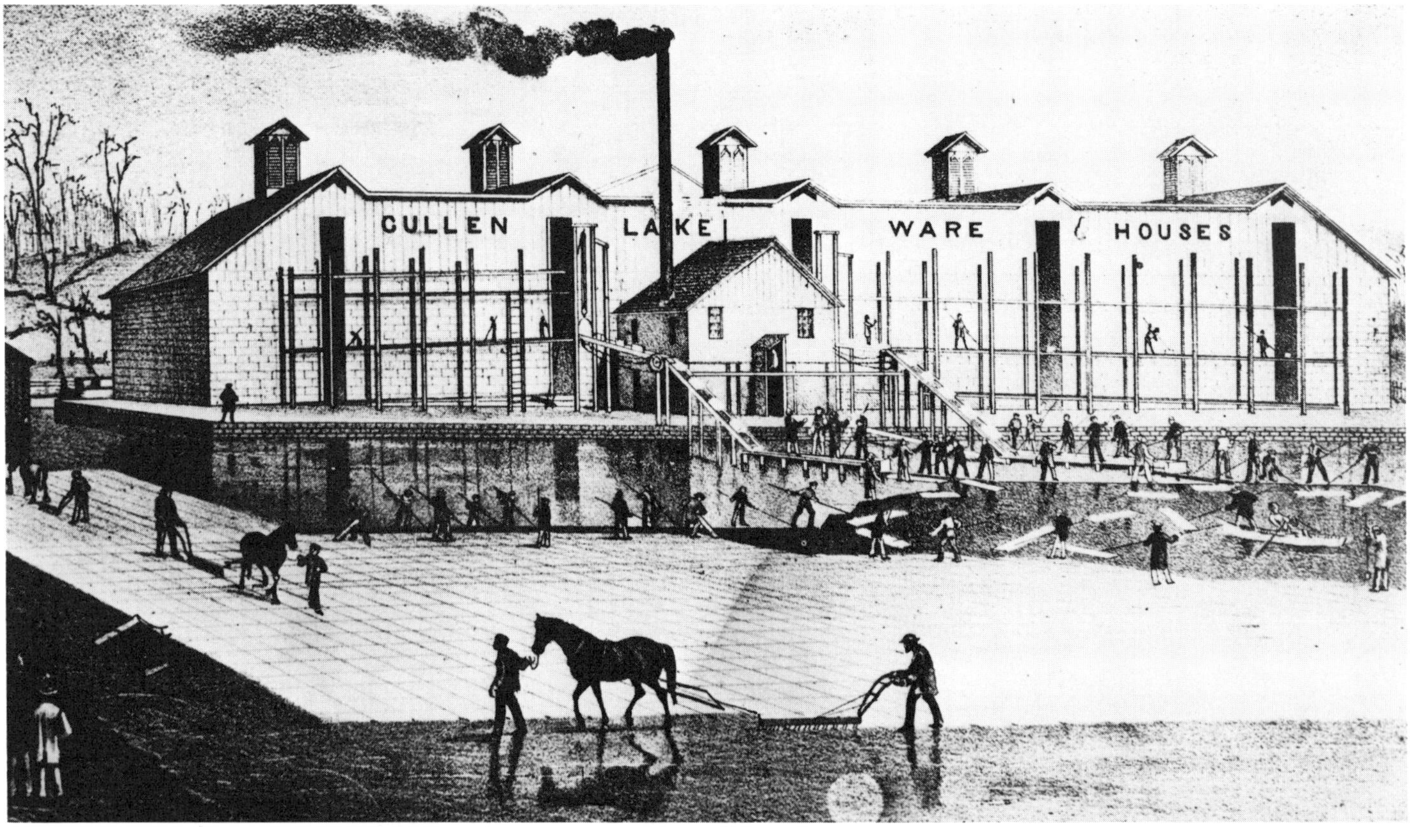
CULLEN LAKE WARE & HOUSES

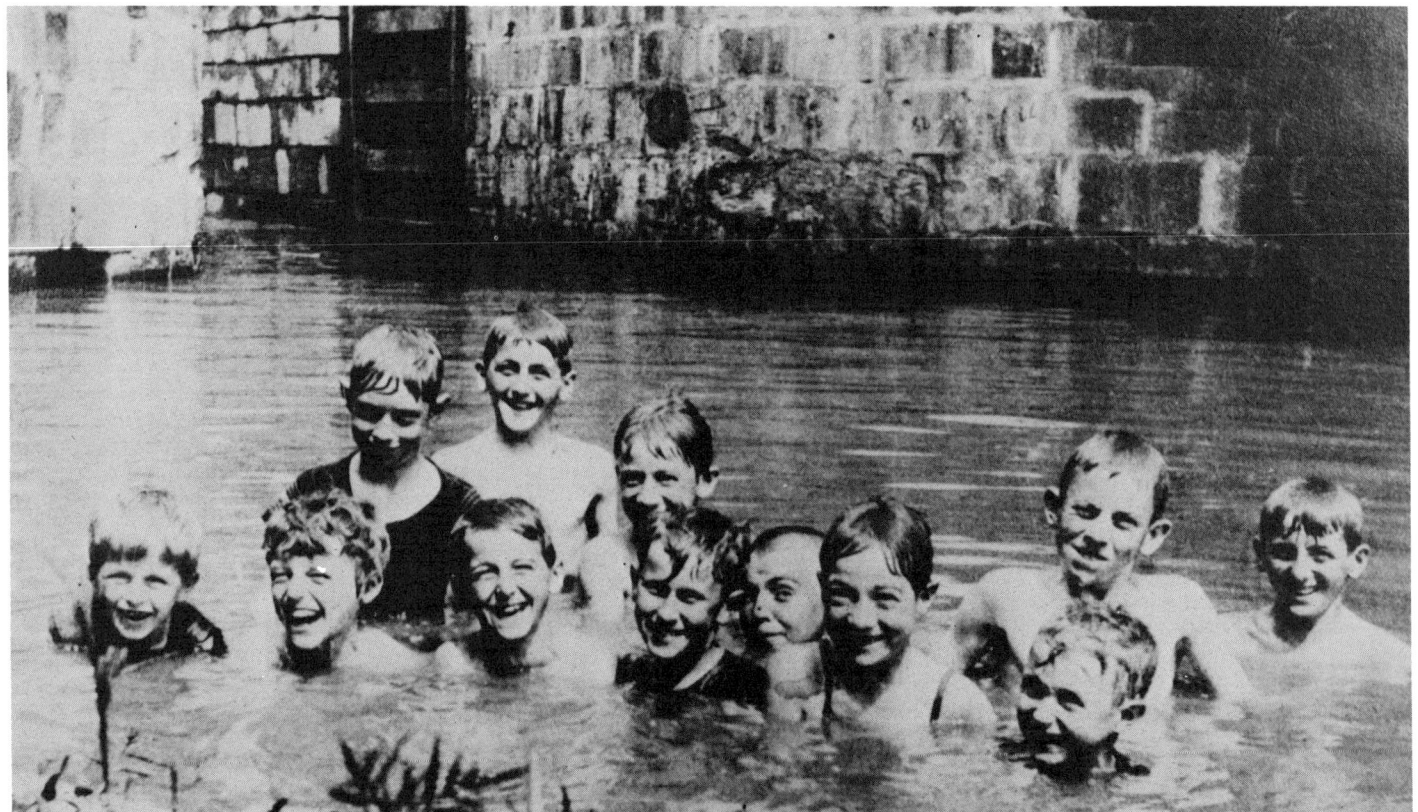

Top left
Hamilton and Middletown were well-situated for the ice-making business, as they were within easy shipping distance of Cincinnati, a major consumer. Between the two cities were several shallow man-made lakes into which canal water was directed. After the water froze it was cut and stored in giant icehouses and packed in sawdust.

Bottom left
Swimming in the canal was a favorite summertime sport of these boys from the Amanda-Excello area around the turn of the century. Depicted in the front row, from left to right, are Thomas E. Jones, Henry Craig, Richard E. McLaughlin, Clarence E. Jones, Paul Craig, George Adrion, and Robert Baxter. In the back row are Robert Butts, Ebenezer McLaughlin, Karl Adrion, Harry Cahill, and P.J. McLaughlin.

and laid rails along the canal from Cincinnati to Middletown. A giant electric engine with twin motors that equaled the power of 80 mules pulled along the tow path. Overhead wires and power stations were erected to power the line. The experiment cost about one and a half million dollars.

Locks had to be strengthened and were either plastered with a layer of cement or replaced. By 1901 the reinforcements were in place, but the faster speed of the "electric mules" caused so much erosion of the earthen banks that the experiment had to be abandoned. Captain Ben Hoffman wrote in *Playmates of the Towpath* about his feelings toward the electric mules:

I loved my regular mules, but I had no use for those electric mules—nothing but a flatcar with a motor to pull the boats with 170-foot steel cable. Work on them was like switching cars in a freight yard. When we had real mules, we could ride till we got tired. That was the life, and you could talk to those mules. They were good company.

The mules came back to the towpaths for only a few years, and for a short time they walked over the railroad ties. On May 5, 1905, the rolling stock was sold to the Cincinnati, Dayton, and Toledo Traction Company.

An experiment using gasoline-powered boats on the Miami-Erie Canal also failed, because the boats made large waves that caused the banks to erode. The Lake Erie and Miami Packet Company had been organized to reestablish canal traffic with a new, modern boat called the *Lady Hamilton*. Without its gasoline engine, the boat continued in use until 1915—the last one on this section of the canal.

On July 22, 1909, a bill was introduced into Congress to convert the Miami-Erie into a ship canal. Nothing came of the bill, but hope for the canal lingered on. On April 1, 1919, Colonel Lansing H. Beach asked the federal government to study the feasibility of widening and deepening the canal. On February 5, 1920, the Ohio Assembly passed the Bellew Bill, which created a commission to plan construction of a new, larger canal over the old right-of-way. In 1923 the Hamilton Club and Middletown industrial interests were still promoting the idea. In 1925 W.H. Johnson of Middletown and John R. Goudi of Cincinnati applied for leases of the canal to build hydroelectric plants, but all efforts to solve the problem of canal usage were finally abandoned. So, on November 2, 1929, the Miami-Erie Canal was officially closed at Middletown, the same location where the groundbreaking ceremony had been held 104 years earlier. One of the greatest transportation parades ever held in the county closed the canal in style.

CHAPTER IV
Down On The Farm

Hogs were once driven down the streets of Hamilton and Middletown to pork packinghouses. Later, hogs were brought to railroad stockholding pens for shipment to Cincinnati, as late as the early 1900s.

THE LAND AND THE CLIMATE There is only so much land good for agriculture in the world, and Butler County was given more than her share. The alluvial valley in which the Great Miami River flows and the valleys formerly occupied by rivers produced this irreplaceable natural resource of fertile soil. The soil is largely decomposed limestone gravel. Some areas of the county have better soils than others, with the poorest being found in the uplands of the northern and western townships. The county is in a region of blue limestone; 70 percent of the rocks are limestone, and 30 percent are shale. The uplands are covered with a sandy loam, and the bottom lands, which constitute 20 percent of the farmlands, represent alluvial deposits left by the river.

The climate is favorable to agriculture. The average length of the growing season is 178 days, which is four weeks longer than in the northern sections of the state, excluding the strip just south of Lake Erie. The mean rainfall is over 40 inches as compared with the 37.5 inches for the state. The mean annual temperature is 53.6 degrees. The mean summer temperature is 74 degrees, and the mean winter temperature is 31 degrees. The typical year has 240 days of sunshine to insure a high average production of crops.

THE HOG The first settlers of Butler County had brought with them razorback or wood hogs. These humpbacked, long-legged hogs often lived off mast, which consisted of acorns, hickory nuts, and other small nuts. The hogs that lived on this diet rarely weighed over 100 pounds. During pioneer days a housewife believed that meat was sweeter if the hog was not so fat.

When there was a surplus of corn, the pioneer began to feed it to his hogs, for it was discovered that corn-fed hogs made the best meat and brought the best market price. Slowly farmers began to improve their stock and in 1823 over 6,600 hogs, each averaging 200 pounds, passed over the toll bridge at Hamilton.

Farmers in Butler County began to import breeds of hogs from Europe. David M. Magie, who lived south of Monroe in Liberty Township, was the most successful. He developed the Magie hog. Other farmers in the area, such as the Harkraders, also experimented in developing better hogs. The Shakers of nearby Warren County entered into the project and finally an improved Magie hog was produced. It was first known as the Butler County hog. After further breeding, the hog was given the registered name of Poland-China. This hog, which could be fattened easi-

In the early part of the 19th century, county farmers were organized in threshing rings. Men went from farm to farm, assisting each of the ring members thresh his wheat. One farmer usually owned the threshing rig and was compensated for its use. The machine shown was owned by Wilson Fall, whose farm was located in Madison Township.

ly, became a favorite, not only of the Miami Valley, but also of the developing West. The Poland-China hog was Ohio's greatest contribution to the production of fine livestock.

The pioneers found that corn was best suited to their Butler County land. It could be planted in hills around tree stumps or girdled trees before the land was completely cleared. Soon there was a great surplus of corn. Since transportation was difficult and expensive, a better profit could be realized if the corn was reduced in bulk. The hog was the perfect machine to do this, for a pig would eat seven pounds of corn and convert it into one pound of meat.

Before the building of the Miami-Erie Canal, hogs were often driven to market. Some hogs were driven east, some were driven north to Detroit, but most were herded down to Cincinnati. During a 12-month period from November 1826 to November 1827 almost 40,000 hogs crossed the bridge over the Great Miami at Hamilton on their way to "Porkopolis." Here the hogs were slaughtered, the hams cured, and the pork cut up and packed in brine to be shipped to the South. Much of this pork was purchased by plantation owners for their workers, thus establishing economic ties between Cincinnati and the South.

During this period other towns along the Great Miami River packed pork. Many farmers butchered and prepared their own pork for market, loaded up a flatboat, and sold their produce in New Orleans.

By the late 1820s Middletown, with a port on the canal, had become a major pork-packing center. It remained so until the 1850s when the railroad destroyed the packing industry by taking live hogs to Cincinnati for processing. Then in the 1870s the packing industry shifted to Chicago, and Cincinnati began to lose its lead.

WHEAT While wheat had been grown in early times, by the 1850s it had become a major crop in Ohio and Butler County. Here it was the most profitable crop. While the preparation of the ground took more care than for corn, farmers were willing to expend more labor on what had become their favorite crop. With the invention of agricultural implements such as the drill and reaper, large crops of wheat could be grown.

Wheat was planted in the fall, often around the corn shocks. Since it was still in the ground in the winter, it was called winter wheat. Two major types of wheat were developed. The hard, red wheat made the best bread flour, and the soft, red winter wheat was best for cakes and pastries. Each community had its own grist mill or flour mill, and the millers ground both types of wheat and sold them under different name brands. Wheat is still grown in the county, including some Durham and white wheat.

Farmers used to get together to thresh their wheat. Each neighborhood usually had one farmer with a mechanical bent, on whom they depended for this chore. He owned a threshing machine, powered by a huge engine, that ran conveyor belts to the separator. It separated the wheat from the straw, as the grain fell through tubes into bushel baskets or sacks. By the 1950s the threshing machine became obsolete when the combine became widely used. It cut the wheat and separated the grain in one step.

Today wheat is still grown on Butler County farms, but in much smaller quantities. Corn has a new competitor, the soy bean, and these two crops vie for first place in production.

SWAMPLAND TO FARMLAND One agricultural area of Butler County was slow in its development. In pioneer days in Fairfield and Union townships there were thousands of acres of swampland, where trees such as ash, sycamore, elm, and oak covered the ground. In these undrained areas mosquitoes found a haven. Pioneers avoided them because mosquitoes meant malaria, a disabling fever. The land was dismissed as of being of little value.

In 1836, after studying the engineer's reports, the General Assembly of Ohio suggested that the Butler County Commissioners levy a tax to reclaim the swampland and make it available for settlement since the soil was believed to be very fertile.

On April 30, 1839, John W. Erwin was appointed by the Board of Public Works of Ohio to mark out the paths for the drains. He found that the swamp area had increased due to the building of the Miami Canal through the area. Before the canal cut across the swamp, its waters had drained into Pleasant Run, a tributary of the Great Miami River. The canal embankment cut off this natural flow, thus adding to the swamp waters that slowly drained into Mill Creek.

Engineer Erwin placed the drains at the proper spots for the swamp and it was drained. The project cost $22,000 of which one-third was paid by the state. In a few years this land, known as Black Bottom, was producing 100 bushels of corn per acre and became one of the most productive areas of the county.

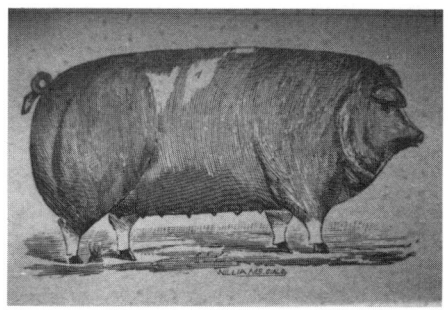

"Lady Pugh," the largest recorded Poland China hog, was raised by William C. Hankinson on a farm near Blue Ball around 1860. It weighed approximately 800 pounds. The Poland China breed was Ohio's greatest contribution to the production of fine livestock. A granite monument, the nation's only such tribute to a pig, is near the county line at Blue Ball.

THE COUNTY FAIR Once the land was cleared and more comfortable log or brick houses replaced crude log cabins, the pioneers found life much easier. By this time the new methods of transportation such as the canal, turnpikes, and railroads opened up world markets and brought increased prosperity to Butler County farm homes.

Farmers began to come together in organizations, for the isolated farmhouses were often lonely places and meetings brought people together. In 1831 the first agricultural society came into being in Butler County. One of its first projects was the sponsoring of a county-wide fair. In 1831 the first Butler County Fair was held in Hamilton. Exhibits included horses, cattle, sheep, grains, vegetables, molasses, wine, and cider. Prizes were awarded to the winners in each category.

The fair attracted farmers and city people alike. At times the farmers resented the towns people's participation, fearing they would take over the rural institution. While horses and cattle were main attractions at the early fairs, farm machinery soon came into the spotlight.

Even the Civil War failed to end interest in the county fair. Though many young Butler County men were in the armed forces, the fair continued since older farmers bought farm machinery to make up for the loss of labor.

THE GRANGE The Civil War brought the end to Ohio's dominance in the agricultural world as the farming center moved westward to the prairies, and the Homestead Act offered a new start for many of the young men of the state. Many from this area rushed to Iowa and other prairie states.

Before the Civil War, Ohio ranked first in the production of wool and corn, second in wheat and cattle, and third in potatoes and oats. By 1870 Ohio found herself reduced in rank, facing competition from the new West and lowered prices. Because it was a leading agricultural producer, Butler County was affected by national trends.

Discouraged by falling prices and reduced political influence as industry became dominant, the farmers decided to form an organization to protect their position. In 1867 the Grange was organized by Oliver H. Kelley of the U.S. Department of Agriculture. S.H. Ellis, a graduate of Springboro's Miami College, became the official promoter of Granges in southern Ohio.

The first Butler County unit was organized in 1871 in Madison Township with Edward Krider as its first master. The West Chester Grange was organized in 1873 with Joseph Allen as its first master. In 1876 a Grange was started at Reily and Oxford, as well as the Hanover Grange at McGonigle. In 1877 Okeana's Grange held its first meeting. Bethany Grange was organized at Princeton in 1884. Others soon followed.

In later years, after reorganizations, the following units remained in operation: Pomona, Morgan, Reily, Hanover, Collinsville, Elk Creek, Poasttown, Monroe, Union, and Fairfield.

The original objectives of the Grangers were social and intellectual. Practical considerations, however, led members to ask legislators for economic and political support for agriculture. The Grangers led the movement toward scientific agriculture, including such methods of diversification of crops and soil conservation. They worked toward reducing production costs. At times they formed cooperatives to cut purchasing costs and to market grain. They also formed insurance companies and published farm magazines.

Farmers' institutes were promoted by the Ohio legislature by an 1890 act. In later years some Butler County farmers joined the National Farm Organization.

THE DECLINE OF FARMING In 1980 it was reported that of the 301,000 acres of land in Butler County, 182,000 were in agricultural production. One hundred years before 293,000 acres had been in farms— 230,000 acres in actual production, with 63,000 acres in forests and uncultivated lands. During this same 100-year period, the number of farms declined from 4,000 to 1,200, but the average size of the farm rose from 90 to 152 acres. The nature of farming also changed; today over half the people living on farms have other jobs to supplement their farm income.

The loss of so much good farm land in the county has become a cause of concern. The land has gone into urban development, covered with homes of those who work in the cities of the Miami Valley. The cities and towns of the county have also reached out to annex rich farmlands. Industries have developed in cornfields as Butler County has become more and more urbanized.

The annual Butler County Fair, first held in 1831 on Hamilton streets, was moved in 1857 to its present site. As the fair's popularity grew, permanent structures were built on the grounds as this 1875 engraving depicts.

CHAPTER V
Business And Industry Develop

In 1849 William Beckett and Francis Rigdon organized the Miami Paper Mill. It grew into one of the largest paper mills, furnishing paper for the state offices in Columbus, and for printing the McGuffey Reader. In 1887 the mill was incorporated as the Beckett Paper Company and is still in operation. Photo by Elsie L. Bates

MILLING The county's first industries developed to serve the needs of the agricultural community. The gristmill, which ground wheat into flour or corn into meal was the most important mill. Daniel Doty owned a small hand mill that he shared with his Dicks Creek neighbors, but manual milling was slow work. The nearest waterpowered gristmill was the Round Bottom Mill at Columbia, a five-day journey by horseback.

In early 1800 a black engineer named Bambo Harris built a gristmill near what later became Miltonville, and for over half a century it proved to be a successful operation. Harris became one of Madison Township's most respected citizens and a member in good standing at the Little Prairie Baptist Church.

A few years later Stephen Vail built three mills on the east side of the Great Miami River. His mills were not in competition with the Harris mill on the west side since there was no bridge across the river until 1832.

Then came what Hamilton historian Jim Blount has described as the county's second wave of leaders. Blount wrote that "their tools were law books, corporation papers, financial projections, surveyor's tools, construction plans, profit and loss statements."

WATER POWER The beginning of modern industry in the county began when Hamiltonian Henry S. Earhart took his idea for a hydraulic power canal to Engineer John W. Erwin, who drew up the plans. The Hydraulic was fed by the Great Miami River. The Hamilton and Rossville Hydraulic Company was incorporated on March 25, 1841. William Bebb was chosen as its first president with Lewis D. Campbell as secretary. John C. Skinner served as engineer for the Hydraulic and also as civil engineer for the city of Hamilton. On January 27, 1845, water ran through the Hydraulic for the first time. John W. Erwin then turned his interests to Middletown. On April 3, 1852, Erwin entered into an agreement with the city of Middletown "to construct a canal or race from the Northern limits of said Corporation through said Water Street . . . as far South as the southern side of Lebanon Street, for the conveyance of water for Hydraulic purposes." By July 4, 1852, water was let into the Hydraulic, and it provided power for a new Erwin paper mill.

Before many years had passed, the Hydraulic had become the industrial center of Middletown. Along its banks, in addition to the paper mill, was a broom-corn factory, a sawmill, a flour mill, a machine shop, and a woolen mill. Soon other paper mills were built on its banks, and Middletown had become the paper city.

The Sorg Paper Company of Middletown, which owns the Hydraulic, still uses its waters in the manufacture of fine papers. The Hydraulic flows through a major city park adding a recreational resource to its industrial value. Before the closing of the Miami-Erie Canal, the Hydraulic could be connected to it, so that boats loaded on the Hydraulic went directly into the canal through special gates.

AGRICULTURAL EQUIPMENT MANUFACTURING Butler County manufacturing began to expand as companies built new agricultural equipment to be used on Miami Valley farms. Many emigrants to the county were from Germany. They brought with them mechanical skills. In 1846 Anthony Tobias started building threshing machines in Hamilton, adding a gleaner two years later. By 1850 Hamilton firms were manufacturing many types of agricultural implements and displaying them at the fair for all county farmers to admire.

In 1846 Clark Lane began the manufacture of saw and gristmills, paper mills, engines, and agricultural machinery. Lane's diary reveals that he shipped the first portable steam engines to Oregon and California. By 1860 seven Butler County companies were making equipment for farmers. Eleven firms were producing wagons and carriages, and over 20 sawmills were cutting lumber. Owens, Lane, and Dyer, a Hamilton firm, won first prize for its threshers and portable steam engines at the 1816 state fair. At the time the company was producing over 1,000 threshing machines and about 500 grain separators and binders a year. At the same fair another Hamilton company, Long, Black, and Alstatter, was awarded the prize for the best cornstalk cutting machine, while Lorenzo L. Langstroth of Oxford was awarded first prize for his movable-comb beehives.

During the same era, P.P. LaTourrette settled in Middletown. He bought a sawmill in Hamilton and set it up in Middletown. He then organized an iron and brass foundry and began the building of paper and tobacco machinery. Middletown was an important center for both of these industries, and LaTourrette prospered. LaTourrette's companies, through several changes in ownership, are known today as Sulzer-Escher-Wyss, Incorporated.

Outside the major cities of the county were many small manufacturing plants. One by one these small firms disappeared as large national trusts took over the agricultural machinery field. New products with national trade names began to appear on Butler County farms, the first being the McCormick Reaper from Chicago.

THE RAILROADS The railroad provided transportation and was a major factor in the county's industrial growth. In 1846 a railroad was chartered as the Cincinnati, Hamilton, and Dayton, but it took five years to complete. Subscriptions had to be obtained, and stockholders had to be found to invest. On September 22, 1851, the first train with passenger cars rolled into the county from Dayton. Middletonians bought tickets and

Top right
Once the most popular chewing and smoking tobacco brand in the United States, Polar Bear brand was manufactured by P. Lorillard. For many years the Polar Bear sign was perched on the corner of the block-long plant. Prospective laborers bound for the factory from the South climbed off the train when the conductor simply called out, "Polar Bear," making the mention of Middletown station unnecessary.

Bottom
At the time when consumers preferred cigars, pipe tobacco, and chewing tobacco to cigarettes, northern Butler County was a major producer of that type of tobacco. This, the largest of 18 Cullman Brothers warehouses, employed 300 persons at Middletown, handling 30,000 cases of tobacco a season.

BUSINESS AND INDUSTRY DEVELOP

41

Above
George Matthew Verity founded the American Rolling Mill Company. This photograph was taken about 1923, and was used as a frontispiece in True Steel. *Verity considered it his best portrait.*

Facing page, top
Brooks built the 210 for the Cincinnati, Hamilton, and Dayton Railroad. The C.H. & D. later became a Baltimore & Ohio subsidiary line running along the Ohio and Indiana border between Cincinnati and Toledo. From White, Early American Locomotives, *Dover, 1972*

Facing page, bottom left
From a modest beginning in 1900 and with energetic George M. Verity as its president, Armco, Inc., grew into Butler County's largest employer, operating plants at Middletown and New Miami. On June 6, 1936, county residents paused to pay tribute to Verity. After a large parade thousands assembled at Sunset Park.

took their first train ride. The next day over 2,000 people turned out in Hamilton to welcome the train, and many bought tickets.

At the time the C.H. and D. was being completed, tracks for the Hamilton and Eaton railroad were being laid. This line ran northwest out of Hamilton where it met the Richmond and Miami Railroad. Eventually these two lines merged and were absorbed by the C.H. and D. The Junction Railroad Company, chartered in 1848, was planned to connect Indianapolis and Cincinnati by making the junction at Hamilton with the C.H. and D. railroad. The C.H. and D. helped finance construction. On July 1, 1872, Middletonians turned out to greet the first locomotive on their new line. Originally chartered as the Cincinnati and Springfield Railway Company, it became the Cleveland, Columbus, Cincinnati, and Indianapolis Railroad, popularly known as the Big Four.

The Civil War brought prosperity to the railroads. For the year 1860-1861 the C.H. and D. Railroad had gross earnings of almost $650,000. After the war, however, the C.H. and D. found it difficult to compete with the emerging consolidated lines. In 1872, the Cincinnati and Dayton Shortline was completed and cut into C.H. and D. profits.

The Pennsylvania Railroad line, at one time the nation's longest, owned the route from Cincinnati to Hamilton. It purchased the Hamilton, Eaton and Richmond Railroad on August 15, 1887. Eventually the Baltimore and Ohio Railroad acquired the C.H. and D. Then it was, in turn, consolidated with the Chesapeake and Ohio. The New York Central took over the Shortline. Later the New York Central and the Pennsylvania merged to become Penn-Central and later a part of the national Conrail system.

By the 1870s county railroad lines were already proving their worth by bringing in raw materials for manufacturing and hauling away finished products. By then the county boasted of 238 shops and factories employing over 1,600 workers who turned out products with an annual value of five million dollars.

THE STEEL INDUSTRY Beginning as the American Rolling Mill Company in 1900, with George M. Verity as its president, the Butler County Armco Steel plant grew rapidly. The company produced outstanding specialty steel products beginning with its rust-resisting iron.

Armco's success in the steel industry resulted from John Tytus' continuous rolling mill. By reducing the cost of sheet steel, the rolling mill made possible the cheap production of a wide range of appliances and automobile parts. Tytus began an industrial revolution in the steel industry and was awarded a place in Ohio's Hall of Fame at the Ohio Historical Society. Using steel to manufacture vaults, doors, safes, and other equipment for banks was the Heming-Hall Safe Company of Hamilton, now known as a subsidiary of Diebold, Incorporated. The Mosler Safe Company, founded in Cincinnati, moved to Hamilton in 1890.

THE PAPER INDUSTRY An abundant and clean underground water supply helped the development of the paper industry in Butler County.

BUSINESS AND INDUSTRY DEVELOP

Above
The three Mosler Brothers organized a safe and lock company in Cincinnati in 1848, but moved to Hamilton in 1890. The Miami-Erie Canal was at one edge of the company's land and the Panhandle Railroad at another.

BUTLER COUNTY

In 1832 J. and J. Graham erected the first paper mill in Butler County at Black Bottom. It was then a developing mill site at a ferry landing point along the Great Miami River, just west of Symmes Corner. The small village was platted about 1850 as Fair Play. Around 1857 a flood along the river washed out the dam, and the mill closed. Sketch by Millicent Bender

Beckett, Rigdon, and Morris, Hamilton's first paper mill, was built in 1848. After various reorganizations it was incorporated as the Beckett Paper Company in 1887. Founded in 1895, Peter G. Thomson's Champion Coated Paper Mill became the biggest single paper mill in the world by 1935 and employed about 20 percent of Hamilton's population. A Butler County native, William Webster, who was born in Liberty Township south of Monroe, invented the first folded paper bag.

Another county inventor made a contribution to the paper industry. Charles W. Shartle, developed the continuous paper beater, which at one time was used in 75 percent of the paper-making plants in the nation. The firm, founded by Shartle, was consolidated with Hamilton's Black-Clawson Company. The importance of the paper industry in the Miami Valley led to the establishment of a paper technology center at Miami University in 1960, with the support of 24 paper companies in the valley.

FINANCIAL INSTITUTIONS During the last century most of Butler County's business and industry depended on local banks for development loans. At first Butler County citizens used banks in Cincinnati. The Bank of Hamilton opened on July 30, 1818, with a capital of $33,062.

Butler County's first bank printed its own paper currency. Its $10 bill carried an engraving of the covered bridge that linked Hamilton and Rossville. Middletown's first bank, Canal Bank, issued its first note in 1840. After it closed, William B. Oglesby and George C. Barritz opened a bank in 1850, still on the same corner and now part of Ohio's Bank One.

In 1863 the National Currency Act was passed by Congress to institute a national system of banking. Butler County's first financial institution organized under the new law was Hamilton's First National Bank. Its charter was dated July 21, 1863, and its first president was Micajah Hughes. His errand boy, Samuel Fitton, later became the bank's president, and Fitton's son followed his father.

On February 20, 1865, the Second National Bank of Hamilton was organized in an old Hamilton home. It later moved to the Beckett block, and in 1875 erected a new home on High Street. The Citizens Savings Bank and Trust Company was opened in 1906 and became the Citizens Bank in 1958. H.A. Rentschler was president until his death in 1941, when he was succeeded by his son, Peter Earl. The Hamilton Dime Savings Bank was chartered April 8, 1897. The Miami Valley National Bank was opened at Hamilton in 1888 but was taken over by Hamilton's First National Bank in 1914.

The First National Bank of Middletown was organized in July 1865 with John Sutphin as its first president and L.D. Doty as its cashier. In 1872 C.F. Gunckel and J.H. Loehr formed the Merchants National Bank. This bank came under the management of Paul J. Sorg and grew into the city's largest bank. In 1919 it merged with the First National, occupied a new building at Main and Central, and still occupies the same building today. In 1980 Middletown's First National merged with Hamilton's First

Facing page
The Canal Museum, a replica of the lock tender's house along the Miami-Erie Canal, is shown here in 1983. Photo by Elsie L. Bates

The Cincinnati, Hamilton, and Dayton Railroad brought prosperity to the county. Its cost of $1.5 million was soon returned to its stockholders. The arrival of the wood-burning locomotive at the Madison Station was always a welcome event.

National to form the First National Bank of Southwestern Ohio.

Thomas McCullough organized the first bank in Oxford as Smiley and McCullough Bank, which eventually evolved into today's Bank One. On December 21, 1901, the Oxford National Bank was organized. Now it is part of the First National Bank of Southwestern Ohio. Monroe's bank, organized in 1905, is now a branch of the same institution. On February 4, 1908, the Bank of Trenton was chartered by community leaders of the area. Due to the Great Depression, this bank was forced to close in 1931 but was able to pay off its debts. On December 5, 1955, the First National Bank of Middletown opened a Trenton branch. In 1960 it moved to its present location in a beautiful old mansion.

THE INSURANCE INDUSTRY In November 1919, a group of young businessmen who had just returned from service formed a company to write insurance policies providing full coverage for automobiles as permitted by a new Ohio law. Before that time automobiles came under separate policies for fire and theft. For some years prior to the war, Howard Sloneker and Ben D. Lecklider had operated the Ohio Mutual Automobile Fire Insurance Association, which in 1915 became the Union Mutual Insurance Company. This company was incorporated into the new Ohio Casualty firm in 1919 when Lecklider and Sloneker were joined in the new venture by Charles Sohngen, S.D. Fitton, and Samuel Goodman. Lecklider was president and Sloneker was vice president and manager. Half of the stock was held by the company's officers and the other half sold to Butler County citizens. At that time Hamilton was considered a good site for such an enterprise, as it was close to the center of a potential insurance market that could include half the autos in the U.S. Ohio Casualty became the first company to write full blanket coverage for an automobile. In 1925 it offered its Mercantile Blanket Policy to cover burglary and robbery on small businesses. In 1939 Ohio Casualty began to write workmen's compensation insurance.

BUSINESS AND INDUSTRY DEVELOP

CHAPTER VI
Spirit, Mind, And Body: The Growth of Local Institutions

Chartered in 1853, Western College was first known as the Western Female Seminary. Its purpose was to give young women a fine liberal education under a distinctly Christian influence. During its first 33 years it was under the direction of Helen Peabody. In 1977 it was incorporated into Miami University. Photo by George Hoxie

RELIGIOUS INSTITUTIONS The development of churches and religious organizations has played a dynamic role in the history of Butler County. In 1800 the Elk Creek Church, organized at Blumfield by Elder Stephen Gard, was Butler County's first Baptist congregation. Later that year the Fairfield-Hamilton church was opened. The log church at Trenton was built on land donated by Michael Pearce, Trenton's founder. In 1801 Elder Gard organized the Prairie Church in Middletown. At about the same time another Baptist congregation was organized at Brown's Run where the congregation worshipped at the cabins of various members. In 1819 the Baptists built a log church at Mount Pleasant, Madison Township. The present brick structure, built in 1836, is still used for worship, making it the oldest church structure in continuous use in the county.

The First Presbyterian Church at Hamilton began in 1801 and is now known as the Front Street Presbyterian Church. Bethel Presbyterian Church at Indian Creek, which began with 33 members in 1815, had grown to 184 in 1825 to become one of the largest rural churches in Butler County. Here William Holmes McGuffey, the famed Miami University professor who compiled his McGuffey Readers, was ordained a minister in 1829. This historic church is maintained by the Butler County Historical Society.

In 1817 James Hughs, a missionary to the Indians, founded the Presbyterian Society in Oxford. His wife and her mother organized the Oxford Female Praying Society. After Hughs' death in 1821, the society discontinued meeting. When Dr. Robert Hamilton Bishop arrived in Oxford as president of Miami University, however, he reorganized the group. In 1833 they erected their first church building.

Middletown's First Presbyterian Church was accepted by the Miami Presbytery in 1819 with the Reverend Francis Monfort as its minister. The Swamp Creek Presbyterian Church at Monroe called its first pastor in 1802. In 1807 it changed its name to Mount Pleasant Church. The Reverend Samuel Magaw began his ministry at Monroe in 1818. With the aid of the educational fund of the presbytery, he founded the Mt. Pleasant Academy for boys; later it became the Presbyterian Academy. It closed in the 1870s.

In 1798 the Reverend John Kobler came up from Kentucky to map out the first Methodist circuit north of the Ohio River. Methodist ministers rode the circuit, preaching in the log cabins of their members. Hamilton

Above
The Hughes School is located in Liberty Township on Princeton Road. This school building, constructed in 1887, replaced a smaller brick structure which dated back to 1842. The present building was renovated by the Liberty Township Historical Society and is maintained as its museum. Adjacent to it is the modern, attractive Liberty Elementary School. Photo by Elsie L. Bates

Facing page, top
The early Baptist and Methodist ministers of Butler County rode the circuit and preached to small groups gathered in a cabin, as this Herbert Fall sketch depicts. As soon as enough people were interested, a small meetinghouse was built.

Facing page, bottom
Typical of the "little red schoolhouse," this building stood at the corner of Main and Manchester streets in Middletown in 1815. In addition to its regular use, on Sundays it served as a church. Social events were also held, such as community sings, spelling bees, ciphering matches, and dramatic programs.

and Middletown were included on the circuit. The Reverend James Grimes called his neighbors to worship at his cabin in 1805. This small group became a stop on the Miami Circuit. In 1829 it built its first church home, the first brick church in Middletown.

The Catholics organized their first church at Cincinnati in 1819, and in 1821 Father Edward D. Fenwick became Bishop of Ohio. After he died, the Most Reverend John B. Purcell became bishop. St. Stephen's Church at Hamilton was constructed under Purcell's direction. The Hamilton church sponsored the founding of many of the present Catholic churches in Butler County.

The first Jewish religious service was held at Cincinnati in 1819. Today two synagogues are located in the county: Temple Beth Sholom at Middletown, and Beth Israel at Hamilton.

The importance of religion to the people of Butler County today is shown by the fact that almost 300 congregations worship at churches distributed throughout the county.

EDUCATIONAL INSTITUTIONS The second major institution desired in all local communities was a school. As soon as a few families were settled in the area, they built schools.

The first school in Butler County was organized at Fort Hamilton in 1793 for children of soldiers and others working around the fort. The teacher was a Scot sergeant. John Ritchie opened a private school on Front Street in Hamilton around 1807. At that time there were no publicly supported schools. Hamilton's next teacher was the Reverend Matthew G. Wallace who used a room in the county jail for class. At Middletown, Master Beers opened the first school in 1805 in an empty room at Vail's woolen mill. The following year the school moved to a log cabin at Yankee Road and Main Street.

In 1825 the state legislature set up school districts that would have the authority to levy a one-half mill tax on property for support. In 1826 in Butler County a board of school examiners established a system of common schools. Soon each township elected school directors whose duty it was to oversee the schools in the township. Schools were frequently built on a one-acre plat donated by a farmer and located near the center of the school district, so no pupil would have to walk over one mile to school.

During the first half of the 19th century, no provisions were made in the state law for high school education, so a system of private schools, known as academies, developed. They were usually sponsored, and often taught, by a minister or church group. By 1840 Ohio had over 70 such institutions.

Around 1827 William Bebb, later to become Ohio's governor, opened his Sycamore Grove Academy for boys. His academy became so famous that it attracted students from Cincinnati and Dayton, as well as from all parts of Butler County. A future governor, William Dennison, and a newspaper editor, Murat Halstead, were in Bebb's classes. In 1835 the

SPIRIT, MIND, AND BODY

51

Hamilton and Rossville Female Academy was opened under a woman's leadership. When boys were later admitted it became known simply as the Academy. Here author William Dean Howells spent some of his early years.

The best known academy director and teacher of the period was Nathaniel Furman. He started an academy at Middletown in 1833. Fifteen years later he moved to Hamilton to direct the Furman Institute. In 1857 Furman purchased the Butler Tavern south of Hamilton and remodeled it into a school.

The first public high schools were located in Hamilton, Middletown, and Oxford. Township students were permitted to attend these schools on a tuition basis. Under the Boxwell law, however, if an eighth grade graduate could pass a special examination, his township board would pay his tuition. This law thus provided for a free high school education for some rural youths. Alexander Boxwell, the Ohio legislator who wrote the law, made up the questions for the annual examination.

The next advance in education was the consolidation of schools, so that rural children could also attend a graded school. In Butler County consolidation began around 1914 or 1915. Provisions had to be made for transportation. Horse-drawn school wagons, and later, motor buses were used. Amanda School in Lemon township grew into the largest elementary school in the state with almost 1,000 pupils, most of whom traveled to school by bus. Building the new consolidated schools required voter support of bond levies. This meant an increase in taxes, so long campaigns were waged to convince voters to approve the levies.

School building could be acquired in cheaper ways. When Union Township needed larger facilities, it received a windfall. E.W. Scripps, the wealthy newspaper magnate, died in 1926. Union Township, where he had maintained his legal residence, received $123,000 in inheritance tax money from Scripps' estate. The trustees decided the township's greatest need was an addition to the high school. But the money could not be transferred to the school district, so the trustees built a structure that could be used as a school. An elegant township hall was constructed and was then rented to the school district for a small fee. The Grange and other community groups also used the hall. The building is still in use, now as an elementary school. Union and Liberty townships have consolidated as the Lakota District.

The changing needs of students resulted in vocational training. Dale Russell Lee, Butler County's superintendent of schools from 1964 to 1978, led the campaign for an improved county program in this field. Both the Hamilton and Middletown city school districts had developed extensive programs in vocational education, but the county program had lagged behind. Finally, in 1976, Lee's dream school opened at 3888 Millikin Road. The school offered a wide variety of vocational courses to all high school students in the county. An evening adult education program was

Right
These two boys were typical of thousands of Butler County boys during the summers of the 1900s. Short pants held up by suspenders, bare feet, and heads topped off with a cap characterized their casual warm-weather look.

BUTLER COUNTY

SPIRIT, MIND, AND BODY

Left
Dr. William E. Smith, author, historian, lecturer, and teacher, was head of the history department and later the graduate school at Miami University. He served at the university for 36 years.

Far left
As a lasting symbol of Miami University's 150th anniversary, the lovely Sesquicentennial Chapel on Spring Street was dedicated on June 7, 1957. The interfaith chapel, with its simple white spire, was described by John D. Millett as "a house of prayer for all people." The next day the first of many weddings, know as "Miami Mergers," took place. Photo by George Hoxie

also available. The Butler County Board of Education named the school in his honor.

The small township district schools have all disappeared. By 1982 Butler County had five city school districts—Hamilton, Fairfield, Middletown, Edgewood, and Talawanda. The rest of the county is under the control of the Butler County Board of Education, which exercises supervisory control over the four local school districts—Ross, New Miami, Madison, and Lakota. The board's executive officer is the Butler County superintendent of schools.

Butler County also provided the environment for the growth of local higher education. The Ordinance of 1787 created the Oxford Township for the purpose of providing support for an academic community in that part of Ohio. On September 1, 1803, surveyors laid the township out, and lots were available with renewable 99-year leases. A corporation collected the money, and the income created a permanent endowment for Miami University, which was established on February 17, 1809. With the exception of a 12-year hiatus from 1873 to 1885, Miami University has offered an excellent higher education program from 1824 to the present.

Miami University later absorbed two female academies. The Oxford Female Institute, later the Oxford College for Women, became part of the university in 1928. The Western Female Seminary, later the Western College for Women, merged with the university in 1977.

Miami University's most famous figure was the legendary William Holmes McGuffey. He compiled the illustrious McGuffey Readers which contained selections from the Bible and world literature. These readers were used by graded schools across the country, and they poured off the Cincinnati presses, finally reaching a total of 130 million copies, a figure exceeded only by the Bible and the dictionary. McGuffey's wide impact earned him the accolade of "Schoolmaster of the Nation."

THE WRITTEN WORD The first newspapers read in Butler County were those picked up in Cincinnati by travelers. The *Centinel of the Northwestern Territory*, the first paper in the Miami Valley, carried the dateline of November 9, 1793. The earliest paper published in Butler County was James McBride's *Miami Intelligencer* in 1814. Between 1814 and 1860 over 20 different newspapers were published in Hamilton. In 1828 the *Intelligencer* was revived by John Woods with Lewis D. Campbell as editor. Taylor Webster published the *Hamilton Telegraph*, which opposed all of Campbell's political views. In 1862 the two papers merged.

The *Telegraph* was later revived as the *True Telegraph*, which in 1870 became the weekly *Butler County Democrat* and in 1886 was issued daily as the *Hamilton Daily Democrat*. In 1891 Homer Gard became its editor and later president. He changed the name to the *Hamilton Evening Journal*. The paper prospered and its building, at Court Street and Journal Square, is still occupied by the *Journal-News*, a consolidated paper.

John M. Gallagher published Middletown's first newspaper, *The*

Middletown Mail, which lasted about a year. Four more papers had come and gone by 1857. In that year the *Western Journal* was born. It developed into the *Middletown Journal* and purchased its rival, the *Middletown News-Signal* in 1932. The latter had been edited by John Q. Baker, who died the very day his newspaper expired. Oxford's press began with the *Chronicle* in 1834. The present-day *Oxford Press* dates back to the 1880s.

By the 1980s the county was served by three major newspapers. Robert E. White, Jr., was editor of the *Oxford Press.* James Blount edited the *Hamilton Journal-News,* and James Mills edited the *Middletown Journal.* Both the Hamilton and Middletown newspapers publish editions circulated under other mastheads throughout the county.

Butler County natives have contributed to America's literary culture. An early national magazine *Littell's Museum,* became the long-lived *Littell's Living Age,* was the creation of Eliakim and Squier Littell of Trenton. In 1891 Albert Shaw founded a popular commentary magazine, the *Review of Reviews,* that he edited for 46 years. Shaw grew up in Paddy's Run (Shandon), graduated from Johns Hopkins University, and had been editor of the *Minneapolis Tribune.*

From Sycamore Grove near Paddy's Run came another noted political writer. Murat Halstead was born in 1829, the oldest son of the oldest son for seven generations, a fact which is supposed to produce an unusual individual. Murat graduated from Farmers' College in Cincinnati. After working on several Cincinnati publications, he became editor and publisher of the *Commercial-Gazette* newspaper. For many years he wrote an average of 3,000 words a day for publication, setting a record of furnishing more copy for printers than any other writer in the history of journalism. As a free-lance writer, Judge James Clark wrote a weekly article for the *New York Ledger.* Judge Clark had married Lottie Moon, who became a special correspondent for the *New York World.* The poems of Hamiltonian Jane McMechan were published by the *Hamilton Telegraph* and later accepted by William Dean Howells for publication in his national magazines. James Woodmansee, a Liberty Township native, traveled across America and Europe reading his long poems. He was a Hamilton resident when he died in 1887.

In Oxford Mrs. Caroline A. Chamberlin wrote many lovely narrative poems, which were published in newspapers and literary periodicals. Her first volume was published in 1853. In more recent years Dr. E.T. Storer of Middletown compiled a delightful, witty book of portrait poems, *They Made the News.* Ridgely Torrence, poet and dramatist of Xenia, attended Miami University and returned to Miami twice as a teacher of creative writing. A contemporary black poet and Middletown school principal, Jean Gear, expressed a personal viewpoint in her book, *Do You Know How It Feels?*

No one who ever lived in Butler County, however, can equal the influence and power once held by the giant of the literary world around the turn of the century—William Dean Howells. Born in Martins Ferry in 1837, Howells moved with his family to Hamilton when he was only three years old. Here his father took over the publication of the Hamilton *Intelligencer,* the county's leading paper at the time. Howells later recalled these days in Hamilton in his book, *A Boy's Town.*

Howell's love of Ohio is recorded in his *Stories of Ohio.* He learned the newspaper trade from his father, and in 1856 he joined the staff of the *Ohio State Journal.* After a period of government service, Howells became editor of the *Atlantic Monthly* and then *Harpers.* He became one of America's leading literary critics, as well as a noted novelist himself. His encouragement launched many writers on their careers, including Paul Laurence Dunbar, the gifted black poet of Dayton.

Though James McBride received little formal education himself and never attended college, he became president of the board of trustees of Miami University. Born in 1788 Franklin County, Pennsylvania, he moved to Ohio and became a clerk. McBride was elected Butler County sheriff in 1813 at the age of 25, an office then considered the most important in the county. Later he was to become mayor of Hamilton.

As a young man, McBride dreamed that Butler County, then largely rural, would one day be a land of towns and cities. Many pioneers were still alive, and McBride listened to their stories and wrote down what he heard. He wrote and rewrote the drafts and produced 3,000 pages of manuscript material relating to the Miami Valley and Butler County. In 1869 his most famous work was published by a Cincinnati printing company under the title of *Pioneer Biography of Butler County.*

McBride also wrote histories of Hamilton and Oxford and a sketch of Miami University, all of which became the basis for the monumental publication, *The History and Biographical Cyclopedia of Butler County* (1882). Another great contribution made by McBride was the production of the county's first map in 1836. A group of local historians combined talents to prepare a *Centennial History of Butler County* using the basic material in the 1882 publication. They updated the information, adding the histories of various communities and the biographies of the county's leaders.

After the publication of the two massive county histories, no others appeared until 1964 when Dr. William E. Smith, in collaboration with his wife, Ophia D. Smith, wrote a definitive history of the Miami Valley. Their notes, which were consulted in the writing of this history, are on file at the Smith Library of Regional History at the Oxford branch of the Lane Public Library. Smith's *History of Southwestern Ohio* fills three volumes and covers the 14 counties that make up the valley.

Another Miami University professor, Dr. Walter Havighurst, wrote many books steeped in regional history, bringing to life the valley's past. His wife, Marion Boyd Havighurst, herself a gifted writer, was his collaborator at times. Havighurst wrote *The Miami Years,* a history of the university, as well as the narrative for the *Miami Album* (1981).

Above
At the age of nine, Herbert Fall displayed his first work in 1900 at the Farmers' Institute in Monroe. He later became a professional medical artist at the University of Cincinnati, where he did illustrations for medical texts. After his retirement he did sketches of the Butler County of his youth, including his favorite, the Miami-Erie Canal. Photo by Elsie L. Bates

Facing page, top
Founded in 1852, Rathman's Drug Store was incorporated in 1939 when Ernest Rathman asked Harry Lewis to be his partner. In 1945 it became Lewis Drugs, and although Richard Lewis still operated the business, the store was in a new location and building. Photo by Kramer Photography

Facing page, bottom
With its 406 beds, Middletown Hospital is the largest in the county, serving not only northern Butler County but neighboring Warren County as well. Established in 1917, the building has been constantly expanded. The earlier section is shown in the left of the picture, and the large parking garage is shown at center. Photo by Harold Kramer

ARTS Butler County has produced some artists of note. George White (1826-1892) was an Oxford native. Some of his best paintings were lost in a fire, but others have survived in art museums. He lived in Hamilton from 1857 until his death. Charles Barrows (1833-1863) was a landscape artist who painted scenes along Four Mile Creek, one of which is on display at Oxford's art museum. He was killed in the Civil War, where he had drawn battle field maps and other sketches.

One of the first artists associated with the Academy of Fine Arts at Cincinnati was Frederick Eckstein. One of his students was Shobal Vail Clevenger of Middletown, who became a leading sculptor of his day. Engravings of his busts of famous Americans have appeared on postage stamps.

In 1886 the Cincinnati Art Academy was opened with Frank Duveneck as its leading instructor. One of his students was Herbert W. Fall of Madison Township, near Middletown. Fall spent most of his life at the University of Cincinnati as a medical artist. In his spare time, and upon retirement, he returned to his art studio on a Madison township farm and recreated the scenes of Butler County's past. Fall's works have been widely reproduced and are enjoyed in many Butler County homes. His line drawings have been used to illustrate an Ohio history school text, and some are included in this book.

Out of St. Clair township came Butler County's first noted photographer. Lucien C. Overpeck was born in 1853, attended the district school in his township, and became a drugstore proprietor at Trenton. Here he developed an interest in photography. He retired and set up a photographic gallery in Hamilton. He helped organize the Ohio State Association of Photographers in 1890.

Bruce Goldflies of Oxford completed a monumental photographic record of the state of Ohio in the late 1960s when he accompanied Dick Perry, also an Oxford resident, as they toured the state to produce the book, *Ohio: A Personal Portrait of the 17th State*. Perry, born and reared in Cincinnati, produced magazine articles and novels as well as history books about southwestern Ohio.

Beginning his career in 1931 at Miami University's School of Fine Arts, George Hoxie became a staff photographer for the magazine *Modern Photography*. He then returned to Oxford to open his own photographic studio. His work gained national and international attention, and established Hoxie as one of Ohio's foremost photographers. Among other 20th century county photographers are Harold Kramer of Middletown, Patrick Brown of Hamilton, and Elsie Bates of Monroe. George Cummins collected county photographs and other historical materials which have been preserved at Lane Public Library.

HEALING The operation of the first hospital in the county was overseen by the Sisters of Mercy, and the name Mercy Hospital was adopted. It opened October 5, 1892. Hamilton saw the need for a new and larger hos-

SPIRIT, MIND, AND BODY

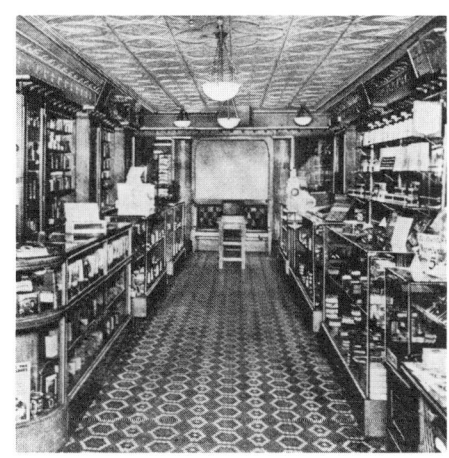

59

The Monroe Historical Society was organized in May 1967 for the purpose of reconstructing this log cabin located on land that was a part of the original Symmes Purchase. Before being dismantled, photographs were taken from every side and each part labeled for later reconstruction. Formally dedicated October 10, 1971, the cabin is used for Historical Society meetings. Photo by Elsie L. Bates

pital and raised the funds to construct a modern structure, so a new Mercy Hospital opened November 22, 1904.

Middletown physicians assigned their patients to Mercy Hospital, but the distance caused problems. After a railroad crash, just west of Middletown, a movement began to raise funds for a Middletown Hospital. In 1913 construction began on the pasture land of the Rager dairy, but wartime demands delayed its completion until 1917. Fort Hamilton Hospital opened in 1928 to serve the city's expanding suburban population. In 1952 the Eugene H. Hughes Memorial Tuberculosis and Mental Hospital opened. These two facilities are now operated as Fort Hamilton Hospital.

Butler County's newest hospital took 20 years to become a reality. In 1958 the Maple Knoll Hospital and Home, on Route 4 in Fairfield Township, asked for permission to convert its maternity center to a general hospital. A survey made at the time revealed the need for such a facility. However, the Greater Cincinnati Hospital Council refused to give its approval, thus eliminating federal funding. In 1972 the Hospital Association of Fairfield was incorporated. This resulted in the construction of a 150-bed facility in Fairfield-Mercy South Hospital. Fifty acres on Mack Road were chosen, and on May 16, 1976, groundbreaking ceremonies took place. Dedication was held two years later, when nearly 6,000 people toured the facilities. In 1957 the new McCullough-Hyde Hospital was opened at Oxford.

PRESERVATION Organized in 1934, the Butler County Historical Society has spearheaded the drive to preserve the county's past. A large 1861 Victorian house, that had been her family's home, was donated by Miss Pauline Benninghofen for use as a museum. The museum now contains works of art, historical artifacts of the county, as well as an extensive collection of books, pamphlets, and manuscript materials. Adjoining the museum at 327 N. Second Street is the Emma L. Ritchie Memorial Auditorium. The hall has served as a meeting place for the historical society since its dedication on May 19, 1968.

One of Ohio's favorite museums is the original home of William Holmes McGuffey. Built in 1833, the house has been restored to its original appearance. The museum even has the octagonal table where the professor compiled his famous readers. The museum contains the most complete collection of McGuffey texts in the nation, as well as other schoolbooks of the last century, many collected by Dean Harvey C. Minnich, former head of Miami's School of Education. The museum is maintained by the university.

The Pioneer Farm and House Museum is operated under license from the Ohio Department of Natural Resources by the Oxford Museum Association. Located in Hueston Woods, the museum features a fine collection of early farm tools and implements in a large barn. The brick farmhouse with twin chimneys was constructed by Joseph Morris in 1832. In 1950 the farm became part of Hueston Woods State Park, and the house was renovated as a museum, opening in 1959. Russell Huston served as its first director.

Ground was first broken at Middletown for the construction of the Miami-Erie Canal in 1825, so the Middletown Historical Society erected a replica of a locktender's house here for its Canal Museum in 1983. The museum contains a collection of canal pictures, many executed by the artist Herbert Fall.

To prevent the possible destruction of an old district schoolhouse on the Princeton Pike in Liberty Township, the Liberty Township Historical Society was organized in 1974. Dedicated to restoring the school to its original condition the energetic group now uses the old school as a headquarters for their activities.

Following the Trenton Sesquicentennial in 1966, a Trenton Historical Society was established in October 1971. The Society opened a museum at 17 East State Street on October 5, 1975. The Monroe Historical Society was organized in May 1967 to assist in the Sesquicentennial celebration of the community. After arranging the observance of the community's founding, the society's first major project was the reconstruction of a log cabin in the Community Park. The log cabin has become a symbol of the municipality. Blue Ball, on the county line, also has an active historical society with a special exhibit at the nearby Warren County Museum in Lebanon.

The idea for a monument to soldiers, sailors, and pioneers began in Middletown in 1895, soon spreading to Hamilton. There a memorial building overlooking the Great Miami was proposed by county officials. In 1898 the state legislature authorized the project, and a county-wide tax levy was approved to assist with both monuments. This photo shows the monument at Woodside under construction in 1900.

CHAPTER VII
Entertainment, Sports, And Recreation

The Sorg Opera House was built in 1890 by Paul J. Sorg to bring culture and entertainment to the area. One of the finest opera houses in the nation, today it presents stage productions and films planned by "The Friends of the Sorg," a non-profit organization devoted to preserving this treasure. Drawing by Herbert Fall

THE PERFORMING ARTS How a society spends its leisure time can be just as significant as the things that that group does to earn a living. Before the media age more people created their own entertainment.

Charles W. Temple had arrived in Oxford in 1820 and traveled throughout the county organizing singing schools. Temple's singers formed the nucleus of the Butler County Musical Association, organized at Hamilton, September 27, 1851. The association's goal was the improvement of church choral music. Presbyterian pastor Reverend John B. Morton was a moving force behind a similar group in Middletown. Oxford, Hamilton, Middletown, and Rossville each had a branch of the association.

The first theater in Butler County was in a barn on Dayton Street in Hamilton. The stage was in the hayloft, and patrons had to climb a wooden ladder to reach the audience area. The stage was illuminated by candle light. In 1821 the Blanchard family of actors appeared and were so enthusiastically received that the following year a Thespian Club was organized. It lasted until 1829 when town officials passed an Ordinance making it unlawful to "publicly act or exhibit any stage play, or stage scene, usually acted in theaters."

The county has been the home of several composers. Western College brought Edgar Stillman Kelley and his wife from Germany in 1910. They were given that college's first fellowship for a composer in residence. Kelley completed several fine works, among them the choral composition, "The Pilgrim's Progress," for the 1918 May Festival at Cincinnati. One of Dr. Kelley's first students, Joseph Clokey (1890-1960), also became widely-known for his musical compositions.

A former trombonist with the Armco Band, Irvin C. Hamilton developed the outstanding Hamilton Municipal Band. In 1936 Eugene Goldflies organized the Middletown Symphony Orchestra, which then performed under the baton of Valda Wilkinson for many years. The orchestra is active as part of AIM, Arts in Middletown, the unified arts organization in that city. The orchestra performs in the elegant Finkelman Auditorium. In 1950 Joseph Bein, a member of the Miami University String Quartet organized the Hamilton Symphony Orchestra.

In 1866 Hamiltonians attended the opening of Dixon's Opera House, which later became the Globe Opera House. The Music Hall was built to compete with the Globe. During the 1890s the Globe and Music Hall vied to bring the best entertainment to the county. In 1899 the Music Hall was

BUTLER COUNTY

ENTERTAINMENT, SPORTS, AND RECREATION

Top left
The interior view of the Sorg Opera House remains much the same as when it first opened in 1891. Although new seats have been installed, the second balcony benches are still in place. The Sorg has one of the only two backstages in the nation with the "Chinese Windlass" still intact.

Bottom left
The old silent movie houses, such as the Jewell, the Jefferson, and the Grand, all operated by Hamiltonian John A. Schwalm, were typical of those of the 1910s and 1920s. The prosperity of the 1920s and the popularity of talking pictures gave rise to such movie palaces as the Paramount Theaters in both Hamilton and Middletown. Photo by Elsie L. Bates

sold to the Hamilton Board of Education and remodeled into Harrison School. In 1903 a new playhouse, the Jefferson, was built to accommodate the traveling stage plays. In 1918 the Jefferson began to present silent motion pictures.

Motion pictures soon overshadowed live theater and vaudeville. In 1919 the Palace Theater was built as an exclusive motion picture house, and in 1920 the Rialto opened. On August 4, 1927 the Rialto presented its first talking picture, a musical called *Broadway Melody*. Talkies were shown at the Palace, the Rialto, the Lyric, and the Paramount.

Middletown's small Bijou Opera House of early years was replaced on September 12, 1891 with the Sorg Opera House, the finest in the Miami Valley. Paul J. Sorg, the owner of Sorg Tobacco Company, was at the time Butler County's richest industrialist. A multi-millionaire, who later became a congressman, Sorg wanted to present a gift to the people of the county. He decided an opera house would bring entertainment and culture. Sorg's wife obtained the finest New York shows offered on the traveling circuit.

The Sorg Opera House had sophisticated stage equipment. The elaborate decorations required some 1,200 electric light bulbs. The stage equipment had a fly tower and a Chinese windlass, which have survived in only one other old opera house in the nation. The theater was also open for political meetings, and many Butler County Democratic functions were held there. Although Sorg was a leading Democrat of the county, Republicans and Socialists also used his theater.

As a live opera house, however, its days were numbered. In 1915 silent motion pictures were run at the end of each performance. On August 4, 1929, the Sorg management announced the last vaudeville program, and on August 6, 1929, it became a movie theater.

Today the Sorg shows films as the Colonial Theater and produces stage productions as the Sorg Opera House. A civic-minded group known as the Friends of the Sorg plan the programs. The theater's owner, Harry Finkelman, maintains the building in excellent repair, and it has been listed as one of the finest opera houses of the nation. Listed on the National Register, the South Main Street Historic District includes the opera house and is backed by an incorporated group known as PRISM.

SPORTS Hunting and fishing have long been popular sports in Butler County. Hunting provided game for the table. Fine catfish were once caught in the Great Miami River. Many fish were plentiful in the Great Miami and its tributaries. As the county became more industrialized, the waterways became polluted. Many of the smaller streams dried up because of deforestation. With pollution control, some fish are returning to county streams. Since 1925 fishing licenses have been required, and this fee helps provide for restocking.

As early as 1808 prizes were offered for winners of horse races on the streets of Hamilton. The winner of the first day won $80, the second day,

$40, and the sweepstakes on the third day. The prizes were made possible by a $4 entry fee. The width of Middletown's Broad Street was determined by its function as a race track. Middletown advertised a race as early as 1823, and the first day's purse was $50. At about the same time, an Oxford promoter promised a $100 prize for a 3-mile race.

By 1836 Butler County had almost 8,000 horses. Many horse races were simple challenges, but this spontaneous racing caused fines to be levied for unsponsored events on roadways and streets. Farmers complained that at the Butler County Fair horse races were becoming the main event. The pacers and trotters overshadowed the farmers' display of their fine work horses.

The first king of harness racing in Butler County was H.D. Kyger. He trained his horses on his own track near Darrtown. His beautiful bay mare, "Kit Curry," which he drove himself, won many races. Kyger had discovered this famous racer, for which he refused a $10,000 offer, pulling a wagon in Eaton. The mare's mother had been one of the horses left behind when General John Morgan was captured. At one time Kyger boasted a stable of 70 race horses.

The first popular lawn game was croquet, which swept the nation in the 1850s. Golf also grew in popularity. A golf course was laid out on the Western College Campus at Oxford in 1898. The president of Armco, George M. Verity, is credited with making the game popular in Middletown, when he laid out a golf course behind his home along the banks of the Great Miami. The Weatherwax Golf Course in Madison Township is one of the areas best planned. Its design provides golfers with six different courses.

Interest in the big spectator sports—football, basketball, and baseball—first developed in the county at the college level. The completion of Herron Gymnasium on the Miami Campus in 1895 gave students a basketball court. In 1904 Miami played its first intercollegiate basketball game with the University of Cincinnati. Soon the "Big Blue" of Hamilton and the Middletown "Middies" were battling it out on the basketball court. Both teams won state championship titles.

The two city teams became rivals on the football field, and the annual Butler Bowl attracted many fans. The first intercollegiate football game played in Butler County was between the University of Cincinnati and Miami University at Oxford. It was played on December 8, 1888. Professors Parrott and Bridgman had organized the football program at Miami. In the game against Cincinnati, Professor Parrott played end, which was not a breach of rules at the time. Bridgman served as referee. Interest in sports increased, and Miami Field hosted thousands of games through the years. Finally the stadium became too small, parking too congested, and a new Miami Field was constructed in 1982. Interest in the Miami Redskins became so widespread that the games have been broadcast since 1949.

In 1861 a baseball game was played at Miami University on a diamond with bases marked by American flags. A runner touching the flag was "safe." Butler County towns soon fielded teams; Oxford, Hamilton, Middletown, and smaller cities all competed. The larger towns joined in the KIO League, which stood for Kentucky, Indiana, and Ohio. A big balloon floated over Middletown on game days. The larger industries in the county also had organized teams that played each other. Baseball and softball are still popular in Butler County, and Little League is a strong summer tradition.

Kenesaw Mountain Landis, America's first commissioner of baseball, was born in Millville. According to a county history, the boy received the odd name from his father, a surgeon with the Union armies, who lost a leg at the Battle of Kennesaw Mountain in Georgia. One "n" was dropped, but the name stuck. Landis participated in sports, including baseball. He attended law school and passed the bar in 1891. In 1905 he was appointed a federal judge. His courtroom manner and decisions brought him national recognition.

In 1915 Judge Landis ruled on a baseball franchise with such sagacity that in 1920 he was asked to become the first commissioner of baseball, a position he held until his death in 1944. He fought corruption in the game, including the "Black Sox" bribery scandal. Landis maintained the respect of players, club owners, and the public. Recognizing the growing importance of radio, he made stations pay for broadcast privileges, and thus strengthened the financial structure of the game. He guided the game through the transportation problems of World War II and helped make baseball the nation's leading summer sport.

PARKS When there was need for a community gathering place, church yards were frequently utilized. Early records of the Mount Pleasant Baptist Church reveal that great dinners were served on saw-horse and board tables, under the oaks and chestnut trees of Madison Township.

Centrally located groves later provided popular meeting places. One such was Doty's Grove at Middletown. Owned by the Doty family, the grove was nevertheless open to the public, free of charge. The Oxford Town Square served a similar function, as did Smith's and Schidman's Sycamore Grove in Hamilton. In the days of the Miami-Erie Canal, Woodsdale Island became a popular resort. Canal boats were chartered to transport groups to various parts of the island for a picnic. These days are recalled in a book by Doris Page and Marie Johns of Trenton.

As Hamilton and Middletown became larger and the county became more urban in nature, parks were laid out as playgrounds for the neighborhood children. Larger parks on the edge of the cities were often established for the employees of a large corporation. Armco Park at Middletown was probably the largest in the county, but the park's 400 acres were deeded to the state in 1966 to become the Middletown campus of Miami University.

Thomson Park in Hamilton is also a company park, maintained by

Street fairs were once a feature of community life. In 1914 A.B. Shetter, whose store was located on North Broad in Middletown, sponsored a farm vehicle and auto carnival, which were the two products he sold.

BUTLER COUNTY

Champion International Corporation for its employees in Hamilton and Middletown. Sebald Park located along Elk Creek in Madison was developed by the city of Middletown in the 1970s as a replacement for Armco Park.

While the cities were developing their own park programs, and Miami University expanding its playing fields, a county-wide program was needed. In November 1955 the Butler County Park Board was organized for the purpose of preserving or restoring some of the county's natural areas. Within 25 years the Board had established 15 parks containing over 700 acres. The County Park Board obtains funds from the county, the state, and individuals or organizations.

Pater Park with the adjoining Bunker Hill Pioneer Universalist Cemetery is the largest Butler County park. A variety of recreational activities are available including fishing. Almost as large an area is contained in Governor Bebb Park in Morgan Township. Named in honor of Governor William Bebb, the Ohio governor's log house is the centerpiece of the park. A covered bridge, originally in use on the Fairfield Road near Oxford, serves as the entrance to the park. The Murstein Youth Hostel, plus two cabins, furnish sleeping space for 50 persons, and a shelter house can accommodate the same number. Hiking trails lead to Dry Fork Creek. The Pioneer Village around Bebb's cabin has grown into a most attractive park area.

Indian Creek Park contains the historic site of an Indian burial ground and an old brick church erected in 1830 and restored by the park board. In the church's old burial ground lie the bodies of Susanna and Thomas Boone, cousins of Daniel Boone. This same area of the county was also the home of a girl who eventually became Mrs. Davy Crockett.

Rentschler Forest preserve joins the Miami-Erie Canal Park and together these make up the county's fourth largest park area. The preserve contains hardwood trees and is typical of the original forest vegetation that the pioneers found when they first arrived in the Miami Valley. The park is also a haven for bird watchers who have sighted over 100 species of birds there. Adjacent to the preserve is the Miami-Erie Canal Park. Here a section of the old canal is maintained. The biking and hiking trail leads north along the old canal route to the Excello Locks Park, where the state's first canal lock can be seen along with its spillway. Across the road from the locks is the old paper-mill town of Excello, with its English-type mill, the Harding-Jones Paper Company, still in operation. Also in the Middletown area is the Miami River Park along State Route 73. It offers a view of the Great Miami, with opportunities for fishing, bird watching, and picnicking.

Park headquarters for the county are at the historic Crawford House in Hamilton, which was built around 1835. The house has been restored with the help of the county's O'Tucks group, representing thousands of community-minded people from Eastern Kentucky who have settled in

The Cummings schoolhouse is one of six log structures that comprise Pioneer Village in the Bebb Forest Preserve. Dry Fork Creek flows through the 174-acre park, where the high bluffs of Ordovician limestone provide scenic topography. John Mundy, chief naturalist of Butler County Parks, and naturalist Bonny Walraven assist "The Pioneers," a non-profit group, in historic programs during the year. Jill Thomas and Kim Sheard of Hamilton posed as students for this photograph. Photo by Elsie L. Bates

ENTERTAINMENT, SPORTS, AND RECREATION

ENTERTAINMENT, SPORTS, AND RECREATION

The Rentschler Forest Preserve joins the Miami-Erie Canal Park. The park features a mile of bikeway along the canal levee, away from the main roads, and a hiking trail on the opposite levee. The forest has deep ravines and excellent wooded areas. Its proximity to the Miami River attracts a myriad of wildlife. Naturalist, author, lecturer, and photographer Will Harbaum is seen here photographing swallows. Photo by Elsie L. Bates

Butler County. The five acres of land surrounding it have been designated the Betsey Newton Memorial Arboretum, where over 120 species of trees may be identified. Another similar facility can be found in Middletown where a private group, in cooperation with the city, maintains the Bull's Run Arboretum for the enjoyment of the public. Lying northeast of Hamilton are two park areas. The St. Clair Recreational Area is near the town of Overpeck. Named after General St. Clair, the park's 26 acres are on the site of an abandoned gravel pit.

In 1973 about 10 acres of land located in Union Township southeast of West Chester was added to the Butler County park system. On Four Mile Creek Road, northeast of Hamilton, is the 16-acre Four Mile Creek Park. Bruce W. Diehl, the county's first park director initiated the development of this first park in the district.

The largest state park in either Butler or Preble counties is Hueston Woods State Park. The park includes 1,600 acres of land and the 625-acre Acton Lake. Walking on the trails reminds one of the days when Johnny Appleseed maintained a nursery nearby. Campsites, cabins, boat launching facilities, hiking trails, and an 18-hole golf course are all available. The Hueston Woods Lodge is a beautiful A-frame structure.

A favorite recreational facility for Butler County youth is Camp Campbell Gard on the banks of the Great Miami River, just four miles north of Hamilton. The 135-acre complex includes: lodges, a recreational center, a swimming pool, a dining hall, a hospital guest house, and the director's lodge. The camp is under the management of the Hamilton YMCA. Camp Hook is a similar youth camp near Middletown.

CHAPTER VIII

Butler County: A Century Of Change

In honor of German immigrants and their descendants' contributions to the development of Hamilton, German Village was established in 1973 by the city council. A walking tour was planned jointly by the Greater Hamilton Chamber of Commerce and Historic Hamilton, Incorporated. Photo by Patrick Brown

At the beginning of the 20th century, census statistics revealed that Butler County had a population of 56,870. By 1980 Hamilton had 62,845 citizens and Middletown had 43,693, and three other towns had grown into cities—Fairfield with 30,816 residents; Oxford, 17,669; and Trenton with 6,375.

Besides these cities there are several unincorporated villages that exist as part of a township; the census listed seven incorporated villages with the following populations: Monroe, 4,259; New Miami, 2,991; Seven Mile, 841; Millville, 811; College Corner, 366; Somerville, 360; and Jacksonburg, 59, the smallest such village in the state. The total population of the county in 1980 was 258,380, representing a growth of 14.2 percent.

Hamilton paced the growth of the county. Near the county's geographical center, Hamilton is located in the Miami Valley, sometimes referred to as the "Ruhr Valley of America." As Hamilton spread out, it incorporated sections of four townships. With a progressive council-manager form of government the city changed from a quiet mid-western town (population 23,914 in 1900) into a thriving industrial center.

During the first quarter of the century Hamilton prospered under its slogan, "Known in World Markets." Corliss steam engines, bank safes, machine tools, stoves, furnaces, and paper products were being shipped to every continent. Hamilton was listed as home to more than 150 companies.

Grace Goulder describes Hamilton as a city that "combines hurrying industry with traditions of another day." The city sponsors an antique car festival each summer. There is a group dedicated to preserving Hamilton's German Village district, a growing tourist attraction. Another group is preserving and restoring Dayton Street with its beautiful mid-Victorian homes, green lawns, and flower gardens. Historic Hamilton, Inc., coordinates the city's preservation efforts from its headquarters in the Lane Hooven House. The downtown section has also been revitalized, centering on the beautifully restored courthouse on High Street. In 1983 an underpass removed the street-level tracks that had stopped downtown traffic.

Throughout its history Middletown has maintained its position as the county's second city. In 1900 the city's main industries were paper and tobacco, with a small Armco Plant turning out its first steel in 1901. The tobacco company ended production in 1951, but the steel industry has grown into a giant, becoming the county's largest employer.

73

Lottie Moon of Oxford became one of the most notorious Confederate spies. A natural actress, she traveled back and forth across the Union lines with ease, carrying vital war information. At one time she crossed the Union lines as a member of President Lincoln's official party. After the war she became a newspaper reporter, lecturer, and novelist until she died in 1895.

Following World War II Middletown's downtown deteriorated rapidly, but the city's leaders refused to let the city die. The National Municipal League gave the 1958 All-America City Award to Middletown with a citation for "progress achieved through intelligent citizen action."

The decade of the 1970s, under City Manager Dale Helsel, saw the downtown business section incorporated into a covered mall. Sound, existing structures served as a basis for the mall design. It is now possible for a person to shop without being exposed to inclement weather. Despite its modern core, Middletown retains the best of its past as a river and canal port.

The roots of Fairfield, the county's third largest city, grew from Fairfield Township, which was created by the state legislature in 1804. After residents of Fairfield Township had watched numerous annexations of township land, they organzied in opposition. The Fairfield Civic Association met on October 28, 1953, and incorporated Fairfield as a village. In 1955 Fairfield annexed the Stockton-Mack Road area. A special census was taken, and the results showed that Fairfield had a population of 6,202, and on October 20, 1955, Fairfield became a city. By 1960 its population reached 14,320. Within a short time Fairfield had a well-organized police and fire department. Its water system was planned in 1956, and a sewer plant was completed in 1967. In 1962 Fairfield received its own post office. A decade of growth followed. The school district grew to include seven modern buildings, with over 7,500 students enrolled. A detailed history of this city has been written by Esther Benzing, Butler County's official archivist.

Oxford was one of Ohio's first planned communities, a rare incident in early American history. A direct creation of the federal government and dictated by the Ordinance of 1787, the town was continued by enabling legislation five years later. The Ohio General Assembly decreed that a town be established around a university. Thus Oxford's origin and growth was linked with that of Miami University. The name Oxford came from the site of the great English university.

The aftermath of the Civil War forced the temporary closing of the university, and the town turned to commercial and industrial activity. One of the first enterprises was a cartographic company operated by Dr. Henry S. Osborn. In 1872 Samuel Tracy, a music teacher, opened an organ plant. A tile plant, a brickyard, two woolen mills, a shoe factory, a drill company, and a chair factory were established before 1900. Today none of these exist, but Oxford has one large manufacturing facility, the Square D Company, and one small one, Alba Manufacturing.

Miami University reopened in 1885 and again became Oxford's major industry. The school's reputation for excellence attracted students from across the country. As Dick Perry wrote, "The university covers over 14,000 acres with brick, students, faculty, and a preoccupation with all kinds of architecture, just so it's Georgian." Perry also added that Oxford is "about the only place you will find a plaque commemorating Lottie Moon, the Confederate spy."

Trenton grew from a population of 847 to become a city on February 13, 1971, with a population of 5,278, adding another 1,000 before the 1980 census. Trenton depended on Middletown industry to provide some employment opportunities. Beginning in 1980 the Miller Brewing Company started construction on the nation's largest brewery at the edge of Trenton in St. Clair Township.

Edward J. Keefe, curator of Trenton's historical museum, has researched the community's past and written a history of it. Alice Hollenbaugh has written a history of Madison Township in which Trenton was formerly located, while Robert Dickey Oglesby and Robert E. Arnett have chronicled the progress of neighboring Lemon Township. Butler County post offices have all been identified by historian Thomas F. Stander. Butler County landmarks are being sketched by Thomas Huff, specializing in the Hamilton area, and by John W. Howard, who often selects scenes from Oxford and Middletown.

WARS OF A CENTURY When Butler County men marched off to the Spanish-American War in 1898 as part of Company E, First Ohio National Guard, some Civil War veterans gave a great farewell for them at Hamilton. This unit, which proceeded under orders to Camp Bushnell at Columbus and Camp Thomas in Tennessee, never reached Cuba.

Another Butler County unit, Company L, First Regiment, Ohio Volunteer Infantry under W.M. Sullivan, also never reached the front and returned to be mustered out at Middletown. Some Butler County individuals who did reach the fighting included Dr. Herbert E. Twitchell, Captain Robert Huston, G.E. Hooven, Charles Stillmacher, Earl Nutt, Wesley Wulzen, Fred Drummond, and John Curran. Jan Hansbrough of Middletown joined a regular army unit, the Ninth Cavalry, an all-black company that was sent to Cuba soon after the war began. The troops of the Ninth Cavalry were with Roosevelt when he stormed San Juan Hill, so Hansbrough was probably the first Butler County soldier to reach the fighting.

Butler County men rallied to the Allied cause in World War I, 17 years later. More than 2,000 of the county's young men joined up and hundreds served overseas as part of the American Expeditionary Force. About 100 county men died in the war. Fourteen Hamilton men enlisted in Battery E, Third Ohio Field Artillery, remaining with the unit when it was transferred to federal service. Another group of county volunteers served in the Armco Ambulance Corps. Among the first to arrive at the French front lines, they rescued the wounded under fire.

One of the three Ohioans to be awarded the Congressional Medal of Honor during World War II was PFC Patrick L. Kessler of Butler County. During the battle of the Anzio beachhead, he killed two German gunners, captured 13 others, and saved his company. In Middletown the American

Patrick L. Kessler of Middletown was one of three Ohioans to be awarded he Congressional Medal of Honor for "conspicuous gallantry" during World War II. The Ohio National Guard Armory at Middletown honors his name as does the auditorium of Post 218, American Legion.

BUTLER COUNTY

Legion auditorium is dedicated to Kessler, and his name also appears on the National Guard Armory located there. Lieutenant George Hook of Middletown served with the Third Army and gained national recognition for his bravery through an article in *Reader's Digest* in June 1945.

In 1963 the United States sent troops to Vietnam. Butler County men were again overseas in uniform. Vietnam became America's longest war, and over 9,600 Vietnam veterans now live in Butler County, the highest per capita concentration of veterans of any county in the nation. Since the founding of the American Legion in 1919, veteran's organizations have influenced Butler County and supported the communities in many ways.

GREAT FLOOD OF 1913 The extended headline of the *Hamilton Daily Republican News* of March 27, 1913, read: "Hamilton Completely Under Water, Miami River Flows Over Entire City from Hill to Hill. Lives Have Been Lost—No List of Dead Available. Property Loss Reaches Many Millions. Water 16 Feet Deep at Third and Market—Fire in Business District.... No Gas, No Water, No Electric Lights and No Communication Possible Anywhere. City Under Control of Troops from Cincinnati and Indianapolis." Before the great flood of 1913 had subsided, the Miami Valley reported property damages of over $300 million, but the loss of 360 lives was far worse.

The month of March 1913 had been marked by unusual atmospheric conditions. On the 13th a storm center formed over the Rocky Mountains; this storm grew worse as it traveled eastward. Southern states experienced tornadoes and flooded rivers. Another storm from the southeast headed toward southwestern Ohio. Sunday night, March 23, the rain began and fell for the next 72 hours. Snowmelt added to the runoff.

The Great Miami River could not contain the volume of water that emptied into it from the swollen tributaries. Troy was flooded, a levy broke at Dayton, Middletown sewers clogged, and, on the morning of March 25, the Great Miami topped its banks at Hamilton. Within a matter of hours almost 75 percent of the city was covered with water.

By the afternoon of March 25, Hamilton officials appealed to the safety director at Cincinnati. A relief party arrived that evening to find flood waters rising at the rate of three feet per hour. It was impossible to reach the downtown area that first evening, so work began in South Hamilton where people were taken from housetops and trees. The next morning rescue work began downtown where the flood waters had reached the tops of the street lights.

Hamilton was a desolate sight. The swift current had taken with it the three bridges that had spanned the river. Streets were torn up and blocked by debris. Some families had fled, others huddled on the top floors for safety. A relief center at the county infirmary treated 1,450 people.

On March 27 a Hamilton Citizens Relief Committee began to coordinate activities. A supply base was established at Central High School, and everything needed was distributed through the committee. The water

This unidentified photo was used as a postcard for many years due to its human interest content. Survivors of the flood watched this horse rescued from the water shortly after the picture was taken.

Facing page, top
Located at the southwest corner of State and Miami streets in Trenton, this building was known around the turn of the century as Blust's Castle. Actually, this building is the remodeled brick house erected in 1801 by Trenton's founder, Michael Pearce. In 1957 the landmark was demolished, making way for a service station.

Facing page, bottom
This 1900 photograph depicts the inside of Rudolph Scheibert's photographic studio in Middletown. Although he later became a teacher, Scheibert continued his interest in photography.

THE CINCINNATI, DAYTON & TOLEDO TRACTION CO.
6

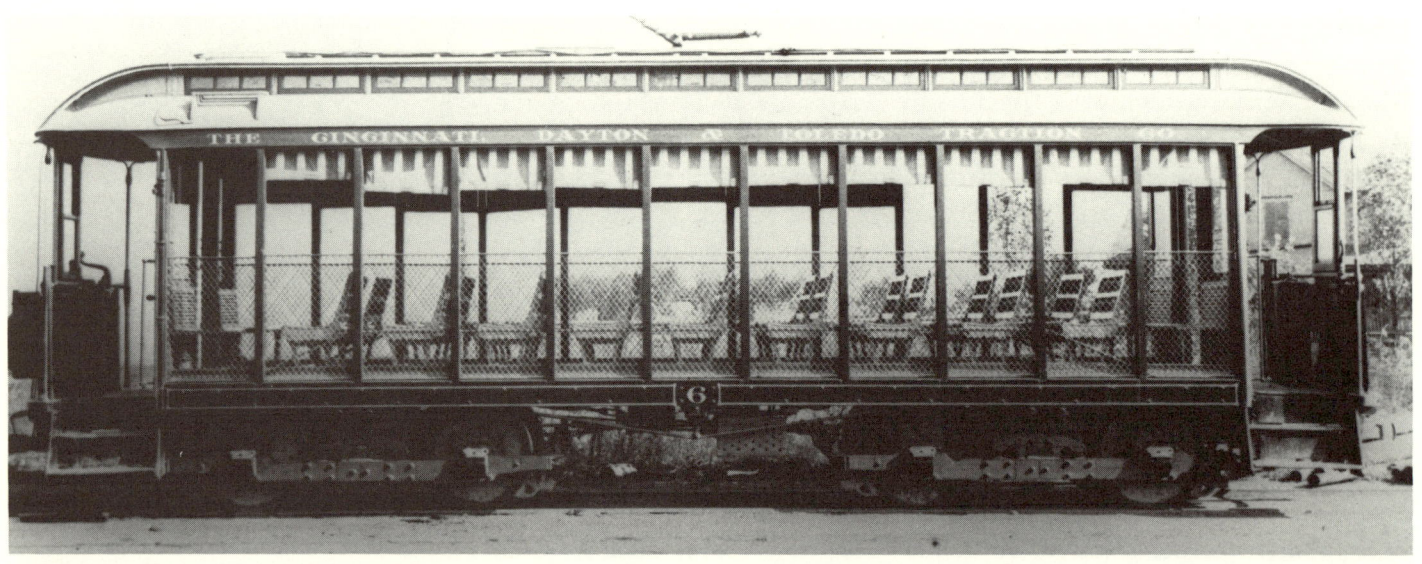

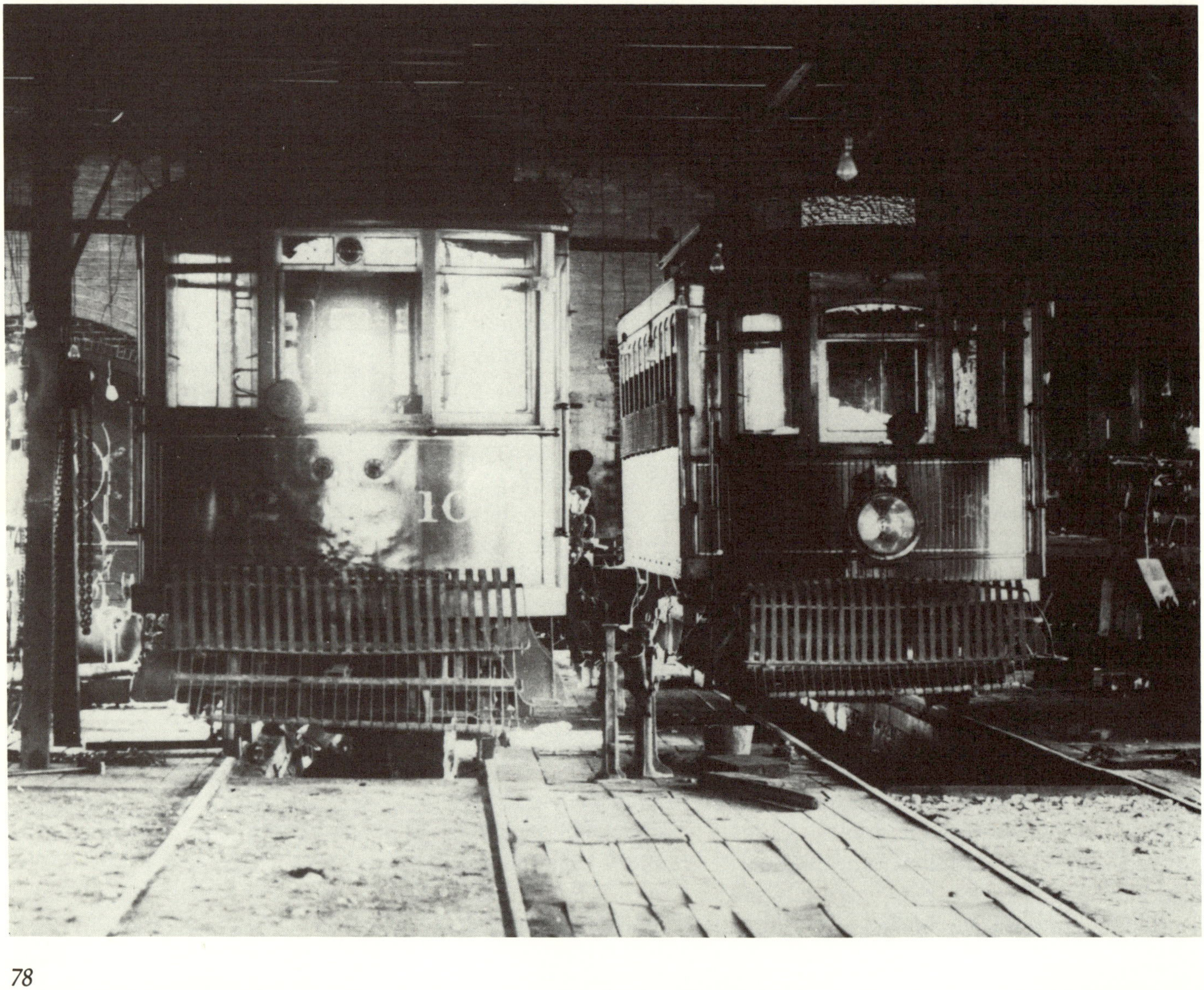
10

subsided, and people returned to the downtown area. On that day, Thursday, Governor James M. Cox declared martial law and three Ohio National Guard units moved into Hamilton. By Friday afternoon funeral services were held for 49 victims of the flood. The final report showed that the Red Cross had assisted 2,094 families with 1,163 receiving furniture, and 360 homes needed repair. Hamilton remained under martial law until May 6. A ferry was used to cross the river, and a temporary pontoon bridge was set up later.

The story in Middletown was similar, except that most of the residents of the flooded area retreated to the hills east of the city, where many stayed with friends and relatives. Middletown was able to care for its own, although relief aid from Cincinnati was appreciated. A unique situation in Middletown sped up the clean-up. The railroad line out of Armco's East Works, not in the flooded area, was connected to the traction line that went downtown. Armco supplied railroad engines and cars, as well as plant workers, to help carry out the debris. The need to prevent future floods resulted in a survey of possible solutions. A meeting was held in Dayton on June 3, and representatives of 13 Miami Valley counties attended. The group chose Arthur E. Morgan, a noted flood-control engineer, to develop overall plans to protect the whole valley. The Ohio General Assembly passed the enabling legislation on February 4, 1914. The flood-control program for the valley that resulted became a model for the nation.

Having a native of the county in the governor's chair during the 1913 Flood helped, and Governor James M. Cox worked tirelessly, first on relief programs then on pushing through the legislation to create the Miami Conservancy District. Cox, born on a farm near Jacksonburg in 1870, moved to Middletown during his high school years, and rose from a newspaper delivery boy to reporter. He gained the attention of Paul J. Sorg, who became a Democratic congressman. Sorg chose Cox as his private secretary. Cox's brilliant record as a three-term governor led to his selection as the Democratic candidate for the Presidency in 1920, but he and his running mate, Franklin D. Roosevelt, went down to defeat.

Only a quirk of fate kept another Butler County native out of the White House. The hotly-contested gubernatorial election of 1891 between McKinley and James E. Campbell was in reality a contest for the Presidency. Two other Butler County men served as governor of the state—William Bebb of Morgan Township and Andrew L. Harris, known as the "farmer statesman."

ROARING TWENTIES While the flood had dampened the spirits of Butler County residents, the removal of their spirits entirely was accomplished by Prohibition, the 18th Amendment, which became law on January 16, 1920. Since pioneer days, Butler County had been a source of hard liquor, with some of its corn crop going into whiskey distilleries. The brewing of beer became a major industry, and Sebald's brewery sup-

Above
James M. Cox, former three-term governor of Ohio, was born on a farm near Jacksonburg in Butler County. He rose from a newspaper delivery boy to reporter to governor. As a running mate in the 1920 Presidential campaign, he and Franklin D. Roosevelt went down to defeat. Cox had worked tirelessly on relief programs during the 1913 flood and then on legislation to create the Miami Conservancy District for flood control.

Facing page
The early traction cars offered few passenger comforts, although this summer car provided an unobstructed view of the countryside in 1900. The line serving western Ohio served Butler County from 1897 until 1939.

Facing page, bottom
The old car barns at Trenton housed and served as a repair station for the cars of the Dayton-Hamilton section of the traction line from 1896 to 1911. This building is now incorporated into the Trenton Magnode plant as the back section of the west building.

plied many Cincinnati saloons. Both towns were a beer connoisseur's dream, with some 27 saloons along Middletown's main street. Prohibition had ended a major Butler County industry.

During the twenties Hamilton acquired the name of "Little Chicago" because of its bootlegging connections to the Windy City on Lake Michigan. Butler County had several roadhouses. While both Middletown and Hamilton police protested that there were no speakeasies in their cities, there were some very close to the corporation lines.

County moonshiners produced their own brands. One man built his still in a rowboat under the floor of a paper mill that had been built over a section of the old Miami-Erie canal. Since police were reluctant to raid the respectable plant, the president of the company evicted the floating still himself. Before the era of lawlessness ended, Clyde Barrows and Bonnie Parker of "Bonnie and Clyde" fame had found their way to Middletown, where Clyde was arrested and spent some time in the local jail.

THE GREAT DEPRESSION AND RECESSION October 1929 brought the spectre of financial crisis. Only those who remembered the Panic of 1893-1897 cut down on spending. County merchants reported 1929 Christmas sales as brisk. As the 1930s began, county industries felt the pinch, and many workers were laid off or cut down to a few hours a week. In 1929 no federal or state programs existed for welfare, unemployment, food stamps, or rent and fuel assistance.

Late in 1930 the state of Ohio began to fight back. The General Assembly passed two bills to assist the Governor's Voluntary Relief Committee. The first substantial aid came through a charity football game held in Chicago in 1931. Ohio received $30,000 which paid for the education of needy children.

In 1932 a new President, Franklin D. Roosevelt, took office and created a number of federal agencies to counteract the effects of the Depression. The Civilian Conservation Corps benefited the county as young men worked with farmers to: plan soil conservation measures, dig drainage ditches, plant trees, and extend roadways. In July 1935 a cadre of 23 men arrived in the county to set up a CCC camp. The first site was the Shafor farm, northwest of Hamilton on the Middletown Pike, but officials discovered that the farm wells could not provide the water necessary for a 214-man camp. The camp was relocated to the Rentschler farm on Milliken and Seward roads, and water was piped in from Hamilton.

The men in the camp sent $25 home each month to keep their families off relief. The workers kept five dollars a month for spending money. Food, clothing, and shelter were provided.

Poverty existed in the county during the 1930s. North and South of Middletown there were settlements along the Miami-Erie Canal where people built temporary housing. Route 73 north of Middletown was lined with such structures. Bean Hollow, south of the city, was a regular shantytown. Poverty was widespread in Hamilton's Peck addition.

Two of 22 entrants in the second annual Fort Hamilton Days "Uprising" are shown above Hamilton. The hot air balloon race began at Miami University and ended in a field north of Seven Mile. Journal-News *photographer Jim Denney took this photograph looking down from another balloon about 1,000 feet over downtown Hamilton.*

BUTLER COUNTY: A CENTURY OF CHANGE

Right
The Benninghofen House was presented to the Butler County Historical Society in 1947 by an heir of the prominent Hamilton industrialist who built it in 1861. The beautifully maintained mansion features Victorian furniture as well as an ornate iron fence and gate, typical of the period. Adjacent to it is the Emma Ritchie Memorial Auditorium, which was dedicated in 1968 to serve not only as a display area, but as a meeting place for the society and historical events. Photo by Elsie L. Bates

Below
The reception hall of the Benninghofen House features the walnut hall tree on the right, which was hand carved in Switzerland. The white and gold vase on the marble top was purchased at the 1890 World's Fair. The Herschede grandfather's clock withstood the damage of the 1913 flood. Photo by Elsie L. Bates

Above
The Benninghofen house parlor is seen here in 1984. On the marble top Belter table are two Bohemian candelabra and one made of crystal. Photo by Elsie L. Bates

BUTLER COUNTY: A CENTURY OF CHANGE

Above
The Sorg Mansion, a Romanesque structure of imported red limestone, was built in 1887 by Paul J. Sorg. The turrets were added in 1902. Gargoyles direct water off the roof. The carriage house is a similar construction, all surrounded by a limestone wall topped with an iron fence. In 1870 Sorg established the P.J. Sorg Tobacco Company. Photo by Pete Lindsey

Left
Originally called "Old Main," this building was the first classroom on the Miami University campus. Remodeled many times, it was eventually called "Harrison Hall," in honor of Benjamin Harrison, an 1852 Miami graduate. Photo by George Hoxie

BUTLER COUNTY

Above
One of the finest old houses in Oxford is Lewis Place, built in 1839 by Romeo Lewis. The platform on top of the house was used in summer to enjoy the cool evening breezes and beautiful view. In 1929 the Lewis heirs sold the house to Miami University to use as a home for its presidents. Photo by Elsie L. Bates

Right
Built in 1863 by Hamilton industrialist Clark Lane, the Lane-Hooven house is located in Hamilton's German Village. Bertrand Kahn bought the house in 1943 and donated it to the community. Listed on the National Register of Historic Places, it houses the offices of the Hamilton Community Foundation and Hamilton-Fairfield Arts Council. Photo by Sutton Landry

BUTLER COUNTY: A CENTURY OF CHANGE

Left
Pat Boryca, head naturalist at Hueston Woods Nature Center, is seen here with "Larry," a great horned owl. Injured and sick wild animals from the area are cared for in the rehabilitation center until healthy and returned to their natural habitats. Those animals which do not recover have permanent homes at the center.

Several generations of the Magie family have successfully operated this hog farm. The Magies raise and sell 1,200 hogs per year on their 300-acre Liberty Township farm, as well as corn, soybeans, and wheat. These piglets represent future income.

BUTLER COUNTY

Top left
The First Marine Band is shown here during a parade in Hamilton, presenting living history in sound. The founder of the unit, Colonel David L. Jaehnig, is an ardent military historian and researcher. He formed the band to recreate the official United States Marine Band that was present during Abraham Lincoln's time. The unit is authentically uniformed, features original instruments for some of its music, and tours internationally. Photo by Elsie L. Bates

Bottom left
Middfest, a colorful annual festival, is held in Middletown's downtown plaza where visitors can enjoy free continuous entertainment and food from many lands. World bazaars offer specialty items from everywhere. Photo by Pete Lindsey

Above
The original structures on historic South Main Street have gone through many changes since their construction in the 1820s. They have been enlarged for growing families, made into apartments, or were restored. Photo by Pete Lindsey

Right
Indian Creek Church in Reily Township was founded in 1810 and built in 1829. Presented by the Indian Creek Cemetery Association to the Butler County Park District in 1960, it was restored by the Butler County Historical Society through the generous gifts of members and friends and dedicated to the pioneers in 1963. It is located on Indian Creek Road where a service is held annually honoring the pioneers of Butler County. Photo by Elsie L. Bates

BUTLER COUNTY

BUTLER COUNTY: A CENTURY OF CHANGE

The Butler County Court House, seen in the left foreground of this photograph, was built between 1885 and 1889. It is an outstanding example of Second Empire architecture and is listed on the National Register of Historic Places. The present clock tower replaced the original cupola which was destroyed by fire in 1912. The Soldiers, Sailors, and Pioneers Monument can be seen in the background. Photo by Elsie L. Bates

Other financial fluctuations followed, and a recession peaked as the 1980s began. Hamilton had experienced an industrial change that began in 1958 and continued into the 1960s with the loss of six industries and over 3,000 jobs.

Steel demand continued to fluctuate with the times, but 1980 found problems developing at Armco, Butler County's largest employer. Although the management modernized the steel plant, foreign steel production made competition difficult. Workers faced layoffs and cuts in wages, but plant profitability began to return in 1984.

In 1970 Hamilton lost population, as did Middletown in 1980. However, the county as a whole showed a increase in population. Educated, skilled leadership promises to keep the county in the forefront. Spearheading this effort are the following groups: the Butler County Private Industry Council; the Butler County Industrial Development Department; the Greater Hamilton Chamber of Commerce; and the Middletown Area Chamber of Commerce.

TRANSPORTATION AND COMMUNICATION The 52-mile section between Cincinnati and Dayton (with Butler County in the middle) was a major link in Ohio's interurban network, stretching 217 miles northward to Toledo. The system began in Hamilton in 1875. The Hamilton Horse Car Line laid double tracks down High Street to the suspension bridge. The horses were slow, so the line raised $100,000 in capital and converted to an electric line, incorporated as the Hamilton Street Railway and Electric Company in the year 1889.

In 1890 the Hamilton and Lindenwald Electric Transit Company opened a two-mile line between the two communities, with service inaugurated on December 17, 1890. According to trolley historian Dan Finfrock of Fairfield, the two Hamilton lines merged in 1898 as the Cincinnati, Hamilton, and Electric Street Railway. Also included in the merger was the Dayton Traction Company and the Cincinnati and Miami Valley Traction line. In 1900 the consolidated company became the Southern Ohio Traction Company with 52.5 miles of track and 29 trolley cars. The line wound its way through Butler County from Symmes Corner to Middletown. Here its tracks went down Main Street to Tytus Avenue, providing the city with a transportation system.

After six mergers, consolidations, and name changes, the line became the Cincinnati and Lake Erie Railroad in 1930. The increasing use of motor vehicles reduced traffic on the C. and L.E. Section by section the line closed, and the last "Red Devil" car ended its final run in Butler County on April 13, 1939. The C. and L.E. became a motor coach and trucking system for a time; the trucks were the first to go, and later the bus franchises were sold. One bus route remained served by the Price Hill lines. However, a federal court case concerning the distribution of the last assets of the company over a valuable right-of-way was finally settled in April, 1983 in favor of Greyhound lines. It represented the oldest pending

Clark Lane, a Hamilton businessman, donated a building and filled it with books for the use of the general public. Lane Public Library opened in 1866, and was taken over by the city of Hamilton in 1867. Photo by Elsie L. Bates

case in the U.S. court system.

The trolley ran on tracks, received its power through overhead electrical wire, and was a feature of the landscape for almost 50 years. The main line in its peak years had direct connections with many other lines, so a traveler could go almost anywhere in Ohio. The cars glided quietly along the tracks, and passengers could watch the countryside roll by.

The first newscast to be heard in Butler County was the KDKA (Pittsburgh) report on the Harding-Cox Election returns of 1920. Since Governor Cox was from Butler County, the news was of great interest. The only area radio system on the air then was WMH, a 20-watt station which had begun broadcasting the previous year from the living room of its owner, Powel Crosley, Jr. During the 1920s local radio enthusiasts were able to receive Dayton and Cincinnati stations.

In 1944 Butler County went on the air with WMOH (its call letters representing Middletown, Oxford, and Hamilton) at 1450 AM. In 1947 Middletown got a professional station—WPFB and later an FM sister. Owner Paul F. Braden used his initials as the station's call letters. Oxford is served by WOXY and WMUB, Miami University. WMOH later built an FM station, which operated independently as WBLZ. WCNW is the 5,000 watt AM station at Fairfield, and WSKS is its FM station. WSKS, formerly as WQMS, was the first FM station in the county. Miami University operates television station WPTO, and WKOI is a local independent station.

South of Middletown in Union Township is a field of 22 antennae and a maze of wires. These are transmission towers for the Voice of America. One of four such installations in the nation, the transmitter is known as the Bethany Station. At any time, day or night, programs are being broadcast, consuming 3.5 million watts—enough electricity to serve a community of 14,000. The 10 transmitters broadcast to Europe, Africa, and South America. The Voice of America speaks in 41 languages to 100 million listeners. Head of this service at Bethany is Charles Stinger, a native of Reily Township.

Early Butler County citizens saw the need for a public library. Efforts were made to establish libraries throughout the county, but volunteers soon tired of the work, and none could stay open. Finally Clark Lane, a wealthy Hamilton manufacturer, established the first public library in the county in April 1866. Two years later the Hamilton City Council received the library as a gift.

Middletown's library facility took much longer. In 1909 a library committee was appointed. Andrew Carnegie offered a grant for a library building, but the city's steel workers disapproved of Carnegie's labor practices. However, local voters approved Carnegie's terms, and in 1913 the library opened.

Lane Public Library has a major branch at Oxford. A 1981 addition houses the Smith Library of Regional History. On January 23, 1983, dedication ceremonies were held for the new 40,000-square-foot Middletown library building at the corner of Broad and Second avenues. The two library systems have divided the county into two parts, with each assuming the responsibility of library service in their assigned area. Each library has its own branches. In the 1980s Douglas J. Bean of Middletown and Mary Pat Essman of Hamilton guided their libraries into the computer age.

ENTERTAINMENT AND SPORTS Some Butler County men and women, each in their own way, enriched other people's lives, not only in the county, but across the nation.

The new Middletown Library became part of a fulfilled dream when it was dedicated January 23, 1983, replacing the outgrown building after 70 years of use.

Frank Simon, a famous cornetist and composer, began his career directing a community band in Middletown. In 1914 he joined John Philip Sousa's band and rose rapidly to become the assistant director. He left Sousa's band and returned to Middletown to organize the Armco Band. Throughout the 1920s the band's reputation grew, and it attracted a national audience each week on network radio. In 1930 Simon hosted the first American Bandmasters Association convention held at Middletown with Sousa in attendance.

During the first part of the century, Lula McClellan, from a Lemon Township family, became a professional whistler. She began with the Armco band, but soon joined the John C. Webbers Band on the Chautauqua circuit, making some 60 appearances each year. Her brother, Robert McClellan, after graduating from the Cincinnati College of Music, went to New York City and performed in opera.

During this same period Louise Todhunter, who shortened her name to Hunter, became an acclaimed prima donna of the Metropolitan Opera Company. After starring in several productions, she signed with Oscar Hammerstein to perform in light opera. Her pioneer forefathers had lived on a farm just north of Monroe, and a road there still bears the family name.

Another talented performer and composer to come from Butler County was Johnny Black. He grew up loving music, learning early to play the piano, violin, and cornet. He was also a poet and published a small book entitled, "Poems and Recorded Thoughts of John Stewart Black." In 1936 he returned to Hamilton opening his own business, the Club Dardanella, now the site of Eaton Manor Restaurant.

In more recent years from the county came the famous McGuire Sisters—Christine, Dorothy, and Phyllis. From Blue Ball, Bonnie Murray rose to grace the operatic stage, and became a featured soloist at many pop concerts. Doris Von Kappelhoff was born in Cincinnati and spent her childhood summers with Aunt Em, Uncle Ben, and Grandpa Felix Bartmann in Trenton. She later changed her name to Doris Day. One of her early professional appearances was at the Butler County Fair.

One of America's most popular novelists of the first half of the century was Fannie Hurst, daughter of Samuel and Rose Hurst, born on Fifth

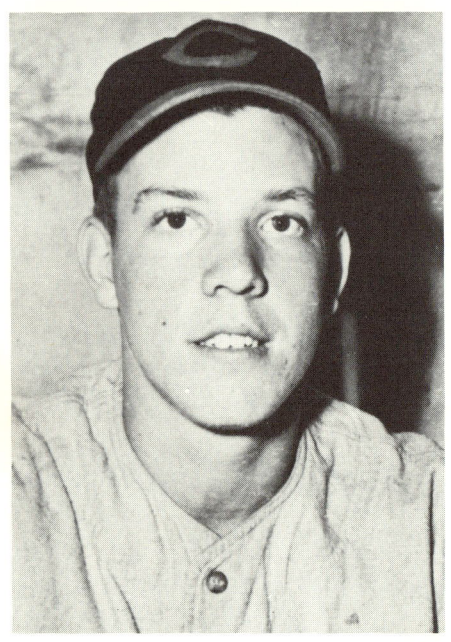

Street in Hamilton in 1889. Many of the scenes and characters in her books are based on Hamilton backgrounds. In 1914 after graduating from Columbia University and touring Europe, Fannie Hurst published her first novel, *Just Around the Corner*. Later novels include, *Lummox, Anitra's Dance, Stardust, The Lonely Parade*, and *Back Street*. *Back Street*, the story of misguided love, was made into a popular movie. For many years, Fannie Hurst was the highest paid writer in the world. She died in 1969.

Butler Countians have always enjoyed sports. To honor local sportsmen the Butler County Sports Hall of Fame was created in 1982. Sports editors Bill Moeller of the *Hamilton Journal-News* and Jerry Nardiello of the *Middletown Journal* were co-chairmen of the project. The charter members who were inducted the first year represent the whole spectrum of athletics.

Charley Root of Middletown, a pitcher for the St. Louis Browns and the Chicago Cubs, won 201 games. Joe Nuxhull signed up for professional baseball when he was only 14. A top Hamilton "Big Blue" athlete, he graduated to the major leagues, spending most of his years with the Cincinnati Reds. Nuxhall became a sportscaster after he retired.

Walter Alston of Darrtown managed the Brooklyn, and later, the Los Angeles Dodgers from 1954-1976. During that time the Dodgers won four world championships and three National League championships. Alston's career culminated on July 31, 1983, when he was inducted into the Baseball Hall of Fame, Cooperstown, New York. Judge Kenesaw Mountain Landis of Millville was baseball's first commissioner.

In football, Weeb Ewbank coached the Baltimore Colts to two NFL championships, and then the New York Jets to a Super Bowl. He began his career at Miami University, which became known as the nation's "Cradle of Coaches." Another famous coach from Miami's cradle was Ara Parseghian, who after coaching the Miami Redskins, moved on to Northwestern and Notre Dame. Paul Walker, who won more state baseball championships than any other Ohio high school coach, piled up 698 wins in 42 years and spent most of his years with Middletown "Middies." One of his players, Jerry Lucas, went on to professional basketball after competing in the Olympic games in 1960. Lynn St. John, as Ohio State University's athletic director, molded the Buckeyes into one of the Big Ten's finest teams.

As a footnote, 1982 marked the end of another epoch in county sports. On November 7 the Miami Redskins played their last game at old Miami Field. After 87 seasons, the field was the second oldest college stadium in the nation. The following September, the team opened its season at Yager Stadium.

Although Butler County has changed through the years, reminders of the past endure. One of these is the Butler County Courthouse. The present structure was opened in 1889, replacing a building erected in 1817 and remodeled in 1837 when a fancy portico and Greek columns were added.

The 1817 structure, in turn, had replaced a simple stone structure built through public subscriptions in 1805. In 1980 a million-dollar renovation was completed, transforming the decaying building into an attractive historic landmark. The building continues to serve some county functions, but it has been supplemented by an elaborate county office building across High Street. The people of the county are proud of their grand old lady in a new dress.

Facing page, top
An accomplished musician, Frank Simon was famous for his dramatic conducting of John Philip Sousa's "Stars and Stripes Forever" and the descriptive music of Ferde Grofé's "On the Trail."

Facing page, bottom
Joe Nuxhall was born and raised in Hamilton where he played baseball with his father and three younger brothers. He played in Knot Hole leagues, in junior high school, and later in a Sunday League, where he was discovered by the Reds at the age of 14. The Reds signed him up at age 15, the youngest player in the major leagues. Courtesy, Cincinnati Reds

Left
Nearing its 100th birthday, the Butler County Court House has been completely renovated. Its interior retains those touches of history marking county milestones, but is also functional. A view from the air also shows the modern county administration building across the street. Photo by Jim Denney

The High Street Underpass in Hamilton is pictured here shortly before its completion. The underpass was a concerted effort by city officials, with the cooperation of citizens, railroads, and the Ohio Department of Transportation. Although plans for this necessary project were first drawn up in 1919, the underpass was a main issue in Hamilton for at least 65 years. Photo by John Janco, Hamilton Journal-News

CHAPTER IX

Partners in Progress
by Thomas Grant and Ercel Eaton

When E.W. Leight opened his Middletown gas station in 1912, gasoline sold for only 11 cents per gallon. His modernized 1919 station is shown in this photograph.

With few exceptions, the first persons to reside in Butler County were the few officers and soldiers stationed at Fort Hamilton in the late 1700s, and routine military activity was the only element of the local economy during those years.

The transition began in the summer of 1794 when General Anthony Wayne's forces defeated the Indians in the Battle of Fallen Timbers. Some of Wayne'e victorious soldiers remained in Butler County, settled near Fort Hamilton, and became farmers and merchants.

Their concerns now were the weather, the heavily forested landscape, the numerous meandering streams, and the pesty wild animals which made pioneer farming difficult. However, these concerns turned to assets which helped Butler County become a prosperous agricultural area and a trading and transportation center.

The fertile soil and adequate rainfall combined with pioneer know-how quickly moved the region from a wilderness and subsistence farming to a settled region producing agriculture surpluses. The rolling terrain and numerous streams, plus an abundance of lumber, encouraged the development of various mills to process the county's harvests.

It was the quest for additional markets which pushed Butler County's development and introduced new businesses and new occupations to the area.

A bridge over the Great Miami, linking Hamilton on the east and Rossville on the west, opened in 1819 and encouraged commerce.

In July 1825 construction began on the Miami-Erie Canal near Middletown, followed by the completion of the waterway through Middletown, Excello, Hamilton, and Port Union to Cincinnati within three years. The canal provided impetus for the industrial growth.

By that time the railroad had also arrived. The first train over the Cincinnati, Hamilton & Dayton line entered Hamilton and West Middletown in the fall of 1851.

Before the middle of the 18th century, less than 50 years after the disappearance of the frontier, it was clear that Butler County's economic base would be diverse. It would include both agriculture and industry, plus the commercial activities which served both elements.

The organizations whose stories are detailed on the following pages have chosen to support this important literary and civic event. They illustrate the variety of ways in which individuals and their businesses have contributed to the growth and development of Butler County. The civic involvement of the area's businesses, learning institutions, and local government, in partnership with its citizens, has made it an exceptional place to live and work.

BUTLER COUNTY HISTORICAL SOCIETY

Fifty years ago, on January 12, 1934, a group of people interested in the history of Butler County met in the Hamilton YMCA and formed the Butler County Historical Society.

The declared purpose of the organization was to assemble the relics and documents of the early days of the county, preventing further destruction and loss of valuable records by people who did not realize their worth.

The Society's founders were Henry Kessling, who called the meeting to order, George C. Cummins, and Michael O. Burns. Dr. Mark Millikin and Walter H. Bruning also attended the meeting. Kessling became the first president of the organization; Cummins was named vice-president; and Charles A. Brennan, secretary/treasurer.

As the Society began to receive historical material, a site committee was formed which included Bruning, Clayton C. Leiter, and Burns as chairman. On March 9, 1934, with the consent of the Grand Army of the Republic (GAR) and the county commissioners, this committee proposed that relics be stored in the Soldiers' and Sailors' Monument. In 1947 Pauline Benninghofen presented her ancestral home, located at 327 North Second Street in Hamilton, as a permanent site for the Butler County Historical Society.

The beautiful Benninghofen home, constructed in 1861, is an example of high Victorian Italianate architecture. In 1874 the structure was acquired by John W. Benninghofen, a local industrialist, who had established a partnership with Asa Shuler, and together they formed Shuler and Benninghofen Woolen Mills.

The home was opened in 1949 as the Butler County Museum. The Society has refurbished the structure, which contains a fine collection of artifacts, works of art, documents, and a genealogy department. The Victorian iron fence and massive corner posts provide an appropriate setting for the picturesque grounds. The home is listed on the National Register of Historic Places.

Adjacent to the Benninghofen home is the Emma L. Ritchie Memorial Auditorium. Mrs. Ritchie, widow of Oscar Ritchie, a prominent industrialist, made the construction of the facility possible in conjunction with the Hamilton Community Foundation.

The auditorium was formally dedicated on May 19, 1968, and is used primarily as a meeting place for the Society and guests. It also houses an additional display area in the basement.

The Butler County Museum is open from 1 p.m. to 4 p.m., Tuesday through Sunday. Tours for groups may be arranged by appointment, and there is no charge for admission.

George C. Cummins (1894-1955), co-founder, was a prominent attorney and historian whose historical collections and records are on display in the Lane Library in Hamilton.

Michael O. Burns (1867-1939), co-founder of the Butler County Historical Society, was prosecuting attorney of Butler County, a judge, and a historian.

Henry J. Kessling, Jr. (1894-1955), co-founder, was an architect, historian, and the first president of the Butler County Historical Society.

COMMUNITY FEDERAL SAVINGS AND LOAN ASSOCIATION

Grover Cleveland was President of the United States when the West Side Building & Loan Association was founded in Hamilton in April 1887.

Alexander Getz had been elected mayor of the city that year, succeeding D.B. Sanders. The rapidly growing community—with a population at that time of 16,000—had completed the union of Hamilton, east of the Great Miami River, and Rossville (on the west of the river).

A suspension bridge erected in 1867 spanned the waterway, serving to further unite the two communities into one city. The town had no electricity; there was a limited supply of gas provided by a privately owned industry, but no streetlighting. Hamilton's own water works supplied factories, stores, and homes. However, there were no paved streets on either side of the river.

The Hamilton Street Railway Company had been in operation since 1875 in the city, promoted and built by Louis Sohngen. Even at that early time Hamilton was becoming an industrial center, hosting many manufacturing concerns.

The city had two daily newspapers, the *Hamilton Daily News* and the *Hamilton Daily Democrat*, plus three weeklies, the *Weekly Telegraph*, the *Hamilton Herald*, and *Die Volks Stimme And National Zeitung*.

The Straub House stood on the northwest corner of Main and A streets, the center of the community's social life. Notables such as P.T. Barnum, William F. "Buffalo Bill" Cody, Clement Laird Vallandingham, and Hamilton native James E. Campbell—Ohio governor from 1890 to 1892—were guests at the inn. However, it was the Beeler Drug Store, at the northwest corner of Main and B streets, where prominent Hamiltonians gathered to discuss the topics of the day.

With the increasing growth of the city and its thriving industry, it became apparent to the devotees of the Beeler Drug Store there was a need for an organization to finance new-home construction. In order to originate such an institution, 1,000 shares of stock at $200 each were issued on April 11, 1887.

The first office was established at the rear of the headquarters of the Temple Medicine Company, at 6 North B Street, and relocated two years later to 9 South C Street, the rear of a gun shop. John L. Beeler became the first full-time executive secretary in 1893, giving up his interest in Beeler Drug; Christ Kaefer was elected president, serving until his death in 1927.

In 1906 the association moved to the Hammerle building at the southwest corner of Main and C streets.

It is well known by all Hamiltonians that Community Federal has played a most important part in the development of the city of Hamilton, allowing the dream of home ownership to come true for more families than any other single lending institution in the community. From its inception the officers, directors, and employees have enjoyed the confidence and respect of the people of Hamilton.

Community Federal Savings and Loan Association (the institution's name since 1983) is still dedicated to the strengths of its founders.

The office of the "West Side" was in the Hammerle building at Main and C streets from 1906 to 1951.

The home of Community Federal Savings and Loan, formerly West Side Federal, at Main and F streets as it looked in 1951.

HAMILTON CASTER & MFG. CO.

Founded on high hopes and entrepreneurial spirit, the Hamilton Caster & Mfg. Co. was begun in 1907 when John Weigel "moonlighted" in a garage behind a friend's Hamilton home.

Eager to develop design ideas and manufacturing techniques for a new line of proprietary casters, Weigel planted the seeds for a business now in its fourth generation.

The enterprise moved to its present location, its third move, to 1637 Dixie Highway following World War I.

In 1928 Hamilton Caster entered the floor truck market by acquiring the H. Zering Manufacturing Company of Cincinnati. That firm's equipment was relocated to a newly constructed two-story building adjacent to the caster plant.

Weigel's son-in-law, Ralph L. Lippert, purchased control of the company in 1937. The new owner's sales-promotion background with a consumer goods company

Years ago Hamilton's caster-manufacturing machinery was driven by line shafts. The cast-iron and malleable-iron caster parts prevalent then have been superseded by steel forgings, weldments, and stampings.

Hamilton Caster employees posed outside their brand-new Dixie Highway plant following World War I. This was the young firm's third location in Hamilton.

enabled him to soon direct Hamilton Caster out of the difficult Depression period.

Two of Lippert's sons had entered the business by the time Towsley Trucks of Cincinnati was acquired in 1963. A third son was associated by the time their father retired in 1976.

Current corporate officers are Lawrence J. Lippert, secretary; Thomas J. Lippert, vice-president; and Robert R. Lippert, president. Dave Lippert, son of Robert R. Lippert, has become the first member of the fourth generation to join the firm.

In the early days most caster components were cast iron, and dimensions were locked in by pattern equipment. Today the use of steel components and modern welding techniques permits the production of different sizes, utilizing common parts. This flexibility can help meet special customer requirements without big tooling costs—for example, by varying caster heights or offsets.

Hamilton Caster has the ability to produce casters and wheels in many non-standard sizes, in special materials such as stainless steel or bronze, and in unique finishes ranging from chrome plating to custom colors.

The name "Hamilton" on a truck or caster has come to be recognized nationally as a symbol of quality, as well as leadership in marketing, advertising, and delivery.

As accurate records of every truck built—standard or special—are maintained, frequent repeat orders are easily duplicated.

Financial stability and fourth-generation management of the family business assure that Hamilton Caster & Mfg. Co. will be there to duplicate an order—three years from now or 30 years—and just as important, to provide parts and service between orders.

Old-fashioned pride of craftsmanship continues at Hamilton Caster.

After enlarging the original plant and constructing an adjacent building for truck manufacturing in 1928, Hamilton Caster occupied its brand-new office building early in 1980. (This photo was taken from virtually the same spot as the original building was pictured.)

HAMILTON ALLIED CORPORATION

When the Great Miami River Valley Flood of 1913 swept through Hamilton, the Sohn and Rentschler Foundry Partnership—founded in 1875 by Henry Sohn and George Adam Rentschler—was obliterated. The operation was totally destroyed, leaving only the building's cupola, the tumbling mills, and the pig iron in the yard.

Prior to the flood the enterprise had prospered, to such an extent that the Hamilton Foundry and Machine Company plant had been formed to handle the overflow work. Built in 1891, that firm acquired the entire business after the original Sohn and Rentschler building had washed away.

The Rentschler name continues to thread its way through the times that have woven the organization into one of the larger, more well-known of its kind in the country. Under the leadership of Peter R. Rentschler, who is chairman and chief executive officer, the company has become Hamilton Allied Corporation; and includes, in addition to its Hamilton plant, a similar facility in Decatur, Indiana.

Hamilton Foundry Division makes ductile iron, gray iron, alloyed irons, and compacted graphite irons, while the Decatur Casting Division is involved in the production of alloyed irons and gray irons.

In addition to the corporate head of the organization, other descendants of George Rentschler who have been associated with the firm include Henry A., Frederick B., Gordon S., and Peter E. Rentschler. Stephen P. Rentschler is the vice-president/sales manager, and James P. Rentschler is vice-president/secretary of Hamilton Allied.

On September 23, 1943, Commander G.H. Bowman, U.S.N., presented the Army/Navy "E" Award to the Hamilton Foundry and Machine Company, stating that it was "the first gray-iron foundry in history to receive the award."

The corporation was the only gray-iron foundry in the country that did no subsequent processing on castings to fly the four-starred Army/Navy "E" flag at the conclusion of World War II. The rigid specifications for quality demanded by that war were no problem to the company, which was following in outstanding performance steps made by its predecessor, the Sohn and Rentschler firm.

Among historical reviews and illustrations in the Butler County archives is the following article, which appeared in the *Republican News* in 1909 (in part): "How this concern has risen step by step from its origin . . . is a tale of individual achievement along foundry lines. It is a story of success and progress. It is a story of the rise of a great industry, happily prospering now and with every indication of a still greater prosperity in the future."

The prophecy of that long-ago writer correctly foretold the coming years for the firm—now Hamilton Allied Corporation. Today one of the larger foundries in the country, it employs about 350 workers and markets its products throughout the nation.

Early workers pose in front of the Hamilton Foundry and Machine Company building, circa 1895.

Known as the S&R Foundry, the Sohn and Rentschler Foundry Partnership was founded in Hamilton in 1875.

PARTNERS IN PROGRESS

FIRST NATIONAL BANK OF SOUTHWESTERN OHIO

With roots firmly set in the two major cities of Butler County—Hamilton and Middletown—First National Bank of Southwestern Ohio today continues its status as the 12th-oldest national bank in the nation, with a tradition of service begun in 1863 by its oldest predecessor bank, the First National Bank of Hamilton.

Both the Hamilton bank and First National Bank of Middletown, chartered on July 12, 1865, prospered in towns that developed along the Great Miami River. Following the Civil War, both banks were to witness a century of unparalleled growth.

The organizers of the two institutions were pioneer citizens of their communities, and many of their descendants are still stockholders of the bank which resulted from their July 1980 merger to form First National Bank of Southwestern Ohio.

Hamilton's original bank (with Charter Number 56) was opened at 239 High Street with Micajah Hughes as its first president. Others involved in the organization were Phillip Hughes, James Beatty, John B. Cornell, Edward Hutchinson, John P.P. Peck, and Joseph W. Davis.

Organized with a capital stock of $100,000, First National Bank of Middletown named Joseph Sutphin, a descendant of the first child born in the village, as its first president. L. Dow Doty, grandson of Middletown's first settler, was the bank's first cashier. Other board members were Francis Tytus, Tobias Lane, S.V. Curtis, William Davidson, Christ Holly, John Shafor, Theo Marston, and J.C. Williamson.

Each of the predecessor banks made numerous moves as they expanded in the ensuing years. And each acquired other smaller financial institutions by merger and by purchase. Hamilton took in Miami Valley Bank in 1914, Dime Savings Bank in 1928, Farmers National Bank of Seven Mile in 1955, and Oxford National Bank in 1961.

Beginning in 1919 the Middletown bank was for a time known as First Merchants National Bank. Then in 1935 this institution merged with American Trust and Savings Bank to become First American Bank and Trust Company. Reverting to its original charter and name in 1943, First National Bank of Middletown made one additional merger in 1953 when it took in Monroe National Bank.

Noteworthy in the Hamilton bank's history is a 1868 quarterly report which boasted that its total resources had reached one million dollars. Nineteen years later the bank acquired a room in a new downtown building at Third and High streets. That facility was razed, and ground was broken for the present eight-story structure in 1929, with occupation taking place the following year.

In 1920 the Middletown bank began construction on a new seven-story banking room and office fa-

The bank's Breiel office in Middletown was completed in 1972. Because of its unique design features, it was chosen as the annual architecture project in 1976 by Miami University.

Robert Q. Millan (left) is chairman, and Richard J. Fitton is president and chief executive officer of First National Bank of Southwestern Ohio.

cility at 2 North Main Street—the city's first tall building. It was opened the following year.

The March 1913 flood brought a muddy current nine feet deep in the Hamilton institution's main banking room. Middletown notes show that no board of directors meeting was held there that March because of flood conditions. And it took several weeks after the flood just to clean the coins and press the bills between blotting paper.

In the early 1920s federal banking laws were amended to permit banks to act as executors, receivers for insolvent business houses, managers of real estate, and negotiators of securities. Both the Hamilton and Middletown banks quickly moved to establish trust departments.

The economy of the city of Hamilton was also hard hit in 1930. Numerous bank closings across the nation drastically reduced orders for machine tools to be produced by local manufacturers. However, no bank or building association in Hamilton closed its doors. And the confidence of the government in the banks of Hamilton was shown when, after the bank holiday of March 1933, the city's financial institutions were the first to receive licenses to reopen.

The early 1950s brought another major change in the life of the banks. With the growth of communities, branching activity was a natural phenomenon. Branching also reached a number of surrounding small communities—Fairfield, Monroe, Oxford, Ross, Seven Mile, Springboro, Trenton,

Originally installed in 1890 in front of the downtown Hamilton office of the bank, this drinking fountain was discarded in 1928. During the bicentennial period the bank and Hamilton Foundry restored it to its original use. The statue on top is Herbe, nymph of streams and brooks. The original work is by Bartel Thorvaldsen (1774-1844) and stands in Copenhagen, Denmark.

A typical teller station, still the heart of banking activity.

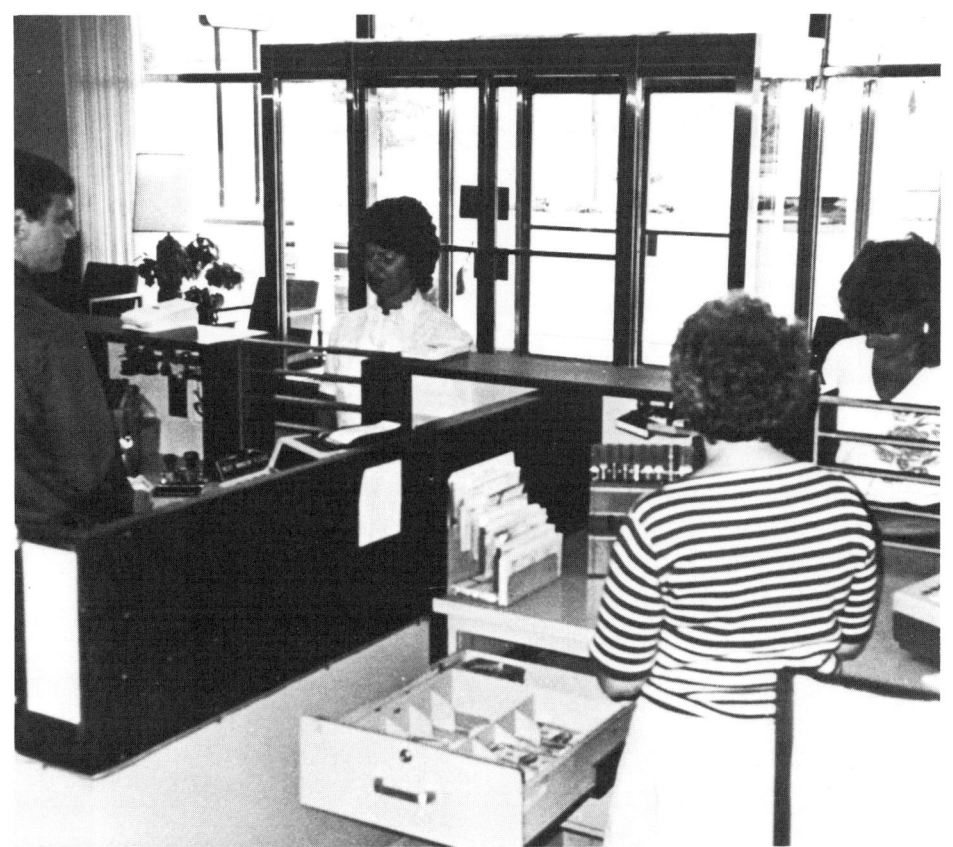

and West Chester.

Since the July 1980 consolidation into First National Bank of Southwestern Ohio, several milestones have passed. Two more banks were acquired: First National Bank in Camden in 1983 and Peoples Banking Company in Lewisburg in 1984.

First Southwestern is also the lead institution in the bank holding company, First Financial Bancorp, which was formed in 1983. First Financial Bancorp also owns Citizens Commercial Bank & Trust Company of Celina.

First Southwestern and First Financial Bancorp are currently led by Richard J. Fitton, who serves as president and chief executive officer. Robert Q. Millan, former president of First National Bank of Middletown, is chairman of the board of directors.

MOSLER
An American-Standard Company

Gustav Mosler left his native Austria to come to the United States in 1854 to seek his fortune. A newspaper editor by profession, he landed in New York with his wife, Greta, and seven children. Later he came to Cincinnati and opened an imported and domestic cigar shop.

At that time a fledgling industry was becoming popular—that of protecting valuables. Mosler went into that business in 1867, and by 1872 Mosler, Bahmann & Co. was one of the biggest safe and lock companies in the world. One of Mosler's early achievements during that period was the design of the famous screw-door burglar safe, which soon drew worldwide acclaim. This unique patented design featured three-movement time locks that eliminated the necessity of lock spindle holes through which explosives could be forced. The world had never seen anything like it.

Repair and service people for Mosler are trained at the William A. Marquard Education Center.

Looking east on Grand Avenue, circa 1900. The stop on the railroad, named Mosler Station, is in the left background.

Gustav Mosler died in 1874, leaving the business to his sons, Moses and William, who then changed the name to the Mosler Safe & Lock Company.

In July 1890 Mosler signed an agreement to move its operation from Cincinnati to Hamilton because of manufacturing space problems and the continuing threat of flooding along the Ohio River. Two prominent local businessmen, O.R. Parrish and Lazarus Kahn, offered $85,000 cash and 40 acres of land, which would later be known as East Hamilton. Ten acres would be set aside for the plant and the remaining 30 acres parceled off into homesites to be sold at "reasonable rates" to Mosler employees.

Production began on October 12, 1890, for the new plant, located on the banks of the Miami and Erie Canal, west of the railroad near Grand Boulevard in Hamilton where the company headquarters still remains.

Not everything was all business at Mosler. A mutual aid society was formed to assist employees during periods of illness and personal distress. A volunteer fire department was formed, and continued in operation even after a city fire station was built. In order to provide power for the plant, private homes, and streetlights, Mosler built a power station called the East Hamilton Power and Light Company. It, in turn, sold power to the City of Hamilton. By this time the business was still flourishing and Hamilton became known as the "Safe Capital of the World."

During the early and mid-1900s Mosler was asked to innovate the security systems that today guard the gold in Fort Knox and protect the Declaration of Independence.

The key to successful innovation at Mosler is the realization that technology is more than factories and ideas. Accordingly, Mosler was one of the first to lead the way in the development of electronic security products. In the past 100 years Mosler has grown from a manufacturer of safes and vaults to a security innovator with sophisticated security applications worldwide.

Recent technology at Mosler embraces cameras, alarm networks, data safes, drive-up systems, currency processing equipment, modular vaults, and other innovations, while at the same time maintaining the values of the worker—giving them the opportunity to provide their families with a secure future.

The objectives of the firm, which is now an operating unit of American-Standard Company, Inc., are still the same but the methods are thoroughly modern. While it is important to remember the lessons of history, the key to Mosler's success is in meeting the security demands of a changing world. Mosler remains committed to the protection of the world's valuables.

It is no surprise that Mosler, with offices in 84 U.S. cities and operations in many foreign lands, is the firm most often selected to solve critically important security challenges—from safeguarding high-rise buildings to protecting automated teller machine networks. It is also no surprise that Butler Countians, when traveling anywhere in the world, can run across a Mosler signature on a security system.

This turn-of-the-century safe is an early example of the firm's product.

This sophisticated Mosler alarm monitors hundreds of security points from one console.

THE HAMILTON TOOL CO.

The year was 1927. The Great Depression had not yet hit when Oscar E. Schlichter and four of his friends got together and founded The Hamilton Tool Co. Schlichter, Fred G. Diesbach, Charles Koehler, Sam Rice, and Joe Wolf had high hopes as they opened their business in Hamilton.

Schlichter, who had been designing printing presses before founding Hamilton Tool, was able to buy out the others and become sole owner of the company by 1940. Manufacturing tools and dies, the venture got under way. In 1929 Schlichter invented an elevating table, which later had the trade name of Portelevator. These tables remained a part of the firm's product line for 50 years.

During World War II Hamilton Tool made high-precision parts for gun sights, manufactured super-sensitive drilling machines, and started making gear hobbers for extremely small gears. But following the war the corporation concentrated on business forms printing presses and collators. In 1946 the company manufactured the first Hamilton web offset press, and in 1947 it produced the first collator.

Hamilton Tool grew from 49 people on the payroll in 1938, to 600 in 1984. It is a locally owned, closely held private company, with the family and relatives of Oscar Schlichter, who died in 1953, as the primary stockholders. Hamilton tool continues to move and refine its products as market needs change, and it has moved into the computer age with energy and zest.

Three plants operate in Hamilton, consisting of 233,178 square feet of space, located on 26.81 acres. Officers of Hamilton Tool are Calvin W. Jung, chairman of the board; Fred H. Harding, president; C. Philip Crampton, executive vice-president; Luther A. Horning, vice-president/customer service; James A. Wilmer, vice-president/production; Kenneth J. Green, vice-president/industrial relations; John M. Cochran, vice-president/production support; James B. Grove, secretary/treasurer; and William A. Kist, controller.

Workers at the original Hamilton Tool plant on South B Street in 1928. From left to right are John Quest, Heinie Seybold, Russell Estridge, Louie Weiss, Gus Schoell, Fred Schlichter, Tom Zoller, John Waldrich, Oscar E. Schlichter, and Kurt Zinnholt.

The current headquarters of The Hamilton Tool Co.

THE LAS-STIK MANUFACTURING COMPANY

Two automobile enthusiasts, Louis C. Sohngen and Martin J. Spoerl, founded the Las-Stik Patch Co. in 1915. Their product was used to repair automobile tire inner tubes.

At the time of the founding both men worked for other businesses, Sohngen in the family bank and Spoerl in the family hardware store. After working hours the two men and their wives cut sheets of rubber to size and put the rubber, a tube of rubber cement, and a metal buffer in a small can. This comprised a tube repair kit.

The demand for their product was there, but the product was not good enough. Realizing this, Louis Sohngen went to Akron where he was able to persuade the B.F. Goodrich Rubber Company into making a three-ply laminated sheet of rubber with the grain of each sheet going in different directions. This new type of rubber sheet was then shipped to Las-Stik for an improved patch, which turned out to be such a success that it wasn't long until Las-Stik moved to larger quarters. Sohngen resigned from the bank in order to devote all his energy to the manufacture and sales of tube patch repair kits.

The firm incorporated in December 1928 as The Las-Stik Manufacturing Company. The purpose was to manufacture accessories used in the automobile trade. By this time, channels of distribution had begun to develop, so sales were directed toward the automotive jobbers. In addition, tire boots and casing plasters were added to the product line and offered for sale.

Louis Sohngen, always interested in something new, developed the Las-Stik polishing cloth. Many changes were made in the formulation of the chemical treatment for the cloth and, as a result, it was soon accepted by motor car companies, oil companies, and many larger retail chain outlets now known as mass merchandisers. Today the cloths are still marketed under the Las-Stik name, as well as under many private-brand labels.

Louis C. Sohngen, founder.

In 1940 Martin Spoerl sold his interest in the firm to Louis Sohngen. Soon thereafter Neil Sohngen joined the business, as did Louis Sohngen, Jr.

During the World War II period, Las-Stik was converted to war production. Because of cloth-handling equipment the company had the capability to produce rifle–cleaning patches. Las-Stik produced 990 million rifle cleaning patches during World War II.

After the war Las-Stik continued as a manufacturer of automotive accessory products. As sales manager, Neil Sohngen discovered that there was a broad need for liquid chemical and lubricating-type products. This brought about the development of many such products, as well as the installation of large-scale compounding and packaging equipment.

In 1984 The Las-Stik Manufacturing Company celebrated its 69th birthday under the management of a third generation. Still operating with the same basic purpose, the firm plans to continue to manufacture and market useful products and to provide needed services.

The Las-Stik Manufacturing Company headquarters, circa 1950.

MERCY HOSPITAL

The imposing front of the 1903 Mercy Hospital, constructed at the end of the institution's first decade in Hamilton. The building housed 70 patients and could be expanded to care for 100 in times of emergency.

The services of Mercy Hospital in Butler County, with added facilities completed in 1984, represent an investment of more than $50 million. That figure is a great distance from that initial payment of $2,500 made to William Hurm for his home on Dayton Street, between Front and Second streets, in 1892.

Hurm reduced his asking price of $9,500 by $250 as his contribution to the new hospital, and gave the institution until July 1894 to complete payment on the property. The Sisters of Mercy, who provided one-fifth of the purchase price of the property, agreed to accept the deed to the property and to run the institution.

With $3,000 the Sisters converted the residence into a place for treatment for 15 patients—complete with an operating room, receiving room, dining room and kitchen, chapel, and sitting room. It was the town's first hospital for a population of about 18,000, with approximately 49,000 residents in Butler County.

Within a few years the adjoining Campbell residence was added to the property. By the turn of the century the institution's services were so much in demand that, in 1903, the trustees decided to build a new hospital. Opening in 1904, the new building on Dayton Street was equipped to handle 70 patients, and in emergencies could be expanded to care for 100 cases. Mercy Hospital continued to expand, adding more and improved health services for residents of Butler County and surrounding areas.

In 1927 a west wing was added; 1948 saw completion of an east wing. A north wing was constructed in 1960 that included an X-ray unit, a surgery department, and a cafeteria. A 1968 enlargement provided for the relocation and expansion of laboratory facilities. Ten years later a new nine-bed intensive/coronary care unit was opened in Hamilton as the latest development in critical care. That same year Mercy opened the county's first intermediate care unit, with 21 beds.

That fall one of Mercy's most ambitious projects—the opening of a new hospital in Fairfield—was realized. More than 5,000 visitors attended dedication and open-house ceremonies in September 1978, as 150 patient beds were shifted to the new facility. As of 1984 Mercy Hamilton had 167 patient beds registered by the State of Ohio, as the facility completed a multimillion-dollar modernization and renovation project approved by CORVA (Health Planning and Resource Development Association of the Central Ohio River Valley).

The new program at Mercy Hamilton includes a new energy center, emergency department, facilities for ancillary services, and the five-story Sister Mary Colette Patient Tower. Prior to the razing of the 1904 building and the old 1928 wing, administrative offices were moved to the renovated east wing.

For the first 14 years of operation, all nursing care was provided by the Sisters, although it was soon evident that additional trained people were needed. This

Typical of Mercy Hospital's efforts to stay abreast of technological advances, this C–T scanner was installed in 1982.

was met in 1906 through the establishment of a school for nurses, where on February 2, 1909, the first two graduates received their diplomas and pins. Today nearly 1,500 employees, in dozens of health care specialties, serve the community at Mercy Hospital.

The nursing school merged into the degree program at Miami University in 1970. However, the hospital continues to conduct two training programs in medical technology and X-ray technology, as well as conducting a Paramedic Training Program certified by the State of Ohio, and serving as a clinical facility for registered and practical nursing students and other allied health students.

Determined to remain in the forefront of medical technology, the institution has continuously updated its equipment and facilities. One of the latest is the completion of the $3.5-million Mercy Ambulatory Surgery Center—a free-standing, outpatient surgical unit located at Mercy Fairfield. Set up as a separate corporation and constructed in keeping with a new trend in health care, the facility is equipped to handle about 90 percent of one-day surgeries normally performed in the conventional hospital.

This friendly lobby at Mercy Hospital opened in 1983 as part of the latest development of the institution, which was founded in 1892.

One of Mercy Hospital's proudest achievements—its new and separate Mercy of Fairfield facility—is shown here in 1978.

The new center eases the load of the hospital's surgery department by freeing operating rooms for more serious cases, and releasing hospital beds for patients staying for extended periods. Another advance in the technological age was gained as the institution added a computerized telephone system between its two facilities, incorporating speed-dialing, call-forwarding, and three-way-conversation abilities. The calls are beamed between the two hospitals by way of microwave dishes mounted on their roofs.

Mercy Hospital is active in numerous community endeavors—helping to fund assistance programs, scholarships, and volunteer efforts through the years. It has been, and continues to be, a vital part of the community that championed its founding so many years ago.

ARMCO INC.

At the turn of the century a man who lived in Kentucky and worked in Cincinnati had an idea. The story of a company, Armco Inc., grew out of a need and that man's idea of how to satisfy that need.

The need was for a reliable source of quality steel sheets to supply a small corrugated steel roofing company. Such sheets weren't easy to come by in the tumult of the emerging steel industry in the United States before 1900. A young man who was manager of a small roofing company formulated an obvious, but yet untried, solution. George M. Verity decided to become his own supplier.

He organized a new firm, ambitiously named The American Rolling Mill Company, and broke ground for its first plant in 1900. It was the first steel company that brought together all the steps necessary to make the steel, roll it flat into sheets, and finally galvanize, corrugate, and fabricate those sheets into a finished product. The first integrated steel firm began with one steel-making furnace, 35 stockholders, and 325 workers. The new idea was not an overnight success.

In the early years of Armco, steelworkers teem (pour) molten steel from a ladle into ingot molds at the original American Rolling Mill Company plant on Curtis Street in Middletown. Open-hearth furnaces refined the steel. At the extreme left is Calvin Verity, son of founder George M. Verity. Just visible to the rear of the ladle is Charles R. Hook, Verity's closest associate. Hook started as night superintendent in 1902 and became president (1930-1948) and then chairman (1948-1959).

Armco's Middletown, Ohio, works of the eastern steel division covers 2,400 acres and currently employs 5,800. The Middletown Works can refine 3.4 million tons of steel annually. It has the capacity to cold-roll 2.8 million tons into finished steel products each year.

It soon became obvious that survival would be based on new markets, new needs, and more new ideas. And it was even more obvious that many of these ideas would come from the men who operated the mill. Later, innovations were to flow from what was to become the first formal research department in the steel industry.

George Verity believed in people, ideas, and success. He developed a management philosophy he called "faith in men." That philosophy meant support for innovators, and it also meant some radical changes in working conditions. The company bought the first steel industry group life insurance policy in 1918. It qualified because of the results of its push for safer working conditions.

In 1919 the corporation formally adopted "Armco Policies," an expression of the philosophy that became the company's code of ethics and a guideline for human conduct for all Armco men and women. These policies are still the firm's standard.

In the 1920s men at Armco were working the first 8-hour days in the steel industry, instead of the 10 to 12 hours that were common in the industry.

One of the most significant accomplishments to grow out of this faith in men was the result of a struggle to develop a continuous

A huge ladle pours molten pig iron at Armco's Middletown Works into the mill's basic oxygen furnace (BOF) to create a 220-ton heat of corrosion-resistant steel for cars and appliances. Armco's 100-millionth ton of Middletown-produced steel was included in the heat. Armco started its original steel-melting operations in Middletown 83 years ago.

National Supply Company, an Armco Inc. group, is the world's largest manufacturer and distributor of oil field equipment. National Supply draw works, pumps, and other equipment provide heart and muscle for this rig drilling in Texas.

rolling process.

In 1924, after years of effort, the process worked. The continuous rolling mill revolutionized the art of rolling sheet steel and made possible the mass production of automobiles and other consumer goods fabricated from steel.

By 1930 Armco had steel plants in Middletown, Hamilton, and Zanesville, Ohio; in Butler, Pennsylvania; and in Ashland, Kentucky. In that year, while in the midst of the Great Depression, the company took a step that was most significant, both for it and for the area.

Armco acquired the Sheffield Steel Corporation. This meant a giant step into new products and a move westward because it added steel-making facilities in Kansas City, Missouri, and a small plant near Tulsa, Oklahoma. And during World War II the company built a major steel-making plant for the U.S. government on the ship channel in Houston.

During the years since that first idea took shape, the concept of faith in men has endured. Innovation and research continue to lead Armco toward better products and better methods.

While steel is still a mainstay in Armco's business, many other industrial activities have been added to the nucleus of steel production. Growth in these businesses, and in steel, reflects an early recognition of the need to constantly search out new and improved products and ideas to meet the needs of customers.

Some 48,000 Armco men and women participate in many diverse business activities. The steel group produces a wide variety of basic carbon steels, electrical steels, and many other specialty and alloy steel products. Armco people in the construction products division fabricate hundreds of

HITCO, a part of Armco's aerospace and strategic materials group, manufactures many space-age products in composite materials. The fluted-core radome being installed on a Boeing 757 protects the airliner's radar against receiving distorted signals.

industrial and construction products from steel and non-metallic materials.

Armco's international activities have grown from a small export business, started in 1911, to an organization of 10,000 people who make Armco products in more than 20 countries, and sell these products and technology around the world.

Founder's Day is a unique tradition with Armco employees. A little more than a year after the death of the man who organized the company, a group of mill workers came to management with a proposal. They wanted to do something to honor the memory of George M. Verity. They knew he believed that "he serves best who serves most."

Each year since 1944, on an April Saturday near the founder's birthday, thousands of Armco men and women at locations around the world organize their own projects and work together to help others.

Ladish Company, a division in Armco's aerospace and strategic materials group, is a world leader in forging technology. At the Cudahy, Wisconsin, headquarters plant, Ladish's 125,000-mkg counterblow hammer forged this 54,000-pound steam chest. Nine feet long and four feet in diameter, it bulks as the largest closed-impression die forging ever made. Westinghouse Electric Corporation ordered the steam chests to govern the flow of superheated steam into electric-power generating turbines.

The modern hot-strip mill at the Middletown Works rolls thick, 19-ton slabs of carbon steel into continuous strips. A series of rollers squeeze the slab and stretch into strips that are, on average, 11-hundredths of an inch thick, 50 inches wide, and 2,000 feet long. After further processing, the flat-rolled steel is sold to automobile and appliance manufacturers.

HOME FEDERAL SAVINGS AND LOAN ASSOCIATION

Home Federal Savings and Loan Association in Hamilton was the fourth such institution founded in the state of Ohio.

Originally called the Home Loan Building Association, it was organized and incorporated on February 21, 1873, by Oakley V. Parrish, James T. Imlay, James E. Griffin, John M. Long, and Harry L. Morey.

Parrish operated an insurance business, and was sales representative for the Singer Sewing Machine Company. He believed that by bringing together people with money to save and those who wanted to purchase homes, a savings and loan association could benefit each.

Home Federal today still operates on the founder's principles. In the minds of many Butler County residents, Home Federal is the Parrish association. There had been a Parrish affiliated with the institution from its inception in 1873 until 1976. O.V. Parrish, the founder, served as secretary, president, or director until his death in 1921.

During his lifetime he was the most prominent man in the savings and loan business in Butler County. Charles J. Parrish, oldest son of O.V. Parrish, joined in 1892 as assistant to his father, and was elected to succeed him as secretary on January 1, 1903. He was elected president in 1939, and served until his death in 1944.

Lee N. Parrish, youngest son of O.V. Parrish, served Home Federal for many years as president. He worked for the organization from 1908 until his death in 1939. Nulton Parrish, only son of Charles J. Parrish, graduated from Miami University and started as assistant cashier. He served as assistant secretary from 1924 to 1939, and as secretary from 1939 until his death in 1959.

Huntington V. Parrish, son of Lee N. Parrish and grandson of the founder, began his career with Home Federal in 1933. He served as president from 1944 until 1964, and then as chairman of the board until his death in 1974. Lee Parrish, son of Huntington V. Parrish, served as director following his father's death in 1974 until his resignation in 1976.

The association's first official place of business was in the third story of the Beckett Block; in 1886 it moved into new offices on the second floor of the Reily Block, a location now occupied by the Second National Bank of Hamilton. In September 1923 the Home Loan and Building Association celebrated its 50th anniversary by moving into a newly constructed building on the southeast corner of Third and Court streets, where it continues to maintain its principal offices.

The first annual statement issued in January 1874 showed assets of $21,600; today the organization has assets in excess of $170 million.

Its positive growth exemplifies the service that the Home Loan and Building Association has provided the citizens of Butler County, and reflects the esteem Hamiltonians hold for Home Federal Savings and Loan today.

The first office of Home Federal Savings and Loan Association. The firm was founded by Oakley V. Parrish, a sales representative for the Singer Sewing Machine Company.

SECOND NATIONAL BANK OF HAMILTON

Saturday, August 29, 1931, was a gala day for the Second National Bank in the city of Hamilton.

That was the day the bank's new building was opened, and it was called "handsome" by the Hamilton *Journal-News*, which was covering the celebration.

Clinton L. Gebhart, bank president at the time, said, "No one can predict the Hamilton of 50 years hence, but we have tried to anticipate the banking needs for our people for that time to come."

Located at the corner of High Street and Journal Square, the structure became Second National Bank's fourth home since its founding on January 19, 1865, in the Hamilton House Hotel, then at the northwest corner of Second and High streets.

Still very visible in downtown Hamilton is this four-story building, featuring a black granite base and the buff tones of Indiana limestone.

Nearly 50 years later the bank's tradition of service excellence continues not only to Hamilton, but to the entire area, with branch banks and drive-in facilities at six locations.

The Second National Bank, known as "the Bank to Grow With," has grown with Hamilton and Butler County since its founding.

The Rossville branch, at 560 Main Street in Hamilton, was the first area bank to install drive-in facilities. Those facilities were built by Hamilton's own Mosler Safe & Lock Company.

The Fairfield branch, located at 563 Patterson Boulevard, was next to open in 1961. Another branch opened in Oxford in 1974 at 1 Lynn Avenue. Three years later a branch in West Chester was built at 9135 Cox Road, and in 1979 the institution's second Fairfield branch was opened at 6550 Dixie Highway.

Alexander Hume was the first president of Second National Bank, and its business was conducted under the direction of William E. Brown, Job E. Owens, John W. Carr, N.C. McFarland, Ezra Potter, and James Rossman.

David McClung, William E. Brown, Charles E. Heiser, John E. Heiser, Clinton L. Gebhart, Bernard H. Geyer, Ned Hitchcock, and Don Litzelfelner have all served as president since that time.

Current members of the board of directors include current president Don Litzelfelner, Ned Hitchcock, Frederic H. Harding, Walter R. Lindsey, Brady F. Randolph, Jr., M.D., John G. Sloneker, and Richard Rogers.

In March 1982 Second National Bank was purchased by First National Cincinnati Corporation.

In 1931 Second National Bank's fourth home was opened at the corner of High Street and Journal Square. This four-story building is still very visible in downtown Hamilton.

The interior of the Second National Bank of Hamilton, located at 228 High Street, in 1901.

PARTNERS IN PROGRESS

BLACK CLAWSON COMPANY SHARTLE–PANDIA DIVISION

One of the largest industrial employers in the Middletown area, the Shartle-Pandia Division of the Black Clawson Company had its beginnings in Hamilton in the 1850s, under the name of Black, Long and Alstatter.

Peter Black and his son, Frank, serviced the paper industry in those early years by installing a roll grinding machine in their shop. Frank Black served an apprenticeship for one dollar a day, in order to become skilled enough to run the roll grinder.

In 1875 Linus P. Clawson found his way into the shop and joined Frank Black in a move that brought the capital needed to increase the stability of the business. It was Clawson's influence and determination that led the firm into what would become its primary endeavor—the building of papermaking machinery. They sold their first paper machine in 1878 to a small mill in Rockdale, Ohio.

In 1926 Black Clawson purchased the Shartle Brothers Machine Company, located on Clark Street, the current site of the Shartle-Pandia Division in Middletown. In the early 1940s Black Clawson's Shartle Division was called upon to produce war material. The quality of workmanship was so recognized that the coveted U.S. Navy "E" Award was presented to the firm for outstanding performance.

And in the 1950s the *Journal-News* editorialized that the firm "has become a world leader in the manufacture of papermaking machinery. Today the Black Clawson Company can manufacture every conceivable type of equipment needed in the preparation of pulp and the manufacture of paper and paperboard." Black Clawson has machines operating in every papermaking country in the world.

The Shartle-Pandia Division of the company is a leader in the development of system technology and complete system instrumentation.

Manufacturing facilities and licenses are located throughout the world, a growth managed and controlled by the Landegger family, which purchased the Black Clawson Company in 1956.

Today the Shartle–Pandia Division of the Black Clawson Company is one of the largest industrial employers in the Middletown area.

The forerunner of the Black Clawson Company had its beginnings in Middletown in 1882. Photo circa 1906.

AERONCA, INC.

From its beginning in 1928, with its first light airplane production, through years of experience in flight that included the outer structure of the Apollo command modules, and on into a transition to a varied mixture of manufacturing, Aeronca, Inc., has kept up with the world.

Aeronca was formed in 1928 by a group of Cincinnati businessmen. Its corporate name was Aeronautical Corporation of America. Taylor Stanley was president, and Robert A. Taft, later a distinguished United States senator from Ohio, was the first secretary.

Among those first airplanes were the C-2, the Collegian, and the Low Wing L. During the '30s the young company had problems with flooding at its original location at Lunken Field in Cincinnati. A decision was made to change locations, and at the same time a name change was made as well. The firm became known as Aeronca Aircraft Corporation.

The move from Lunken to Middletown took place in 1940, and the production of light aircraft continued into World War II. During that time the O-58, L-3, PT-19, PT-23, and TG-5, as well as other aircraft and equipment, were manufactured. Aeronca was the first light plane manufacturer to receive the coveted Army/Navy "E" Award for excellence in defense production, and its quality service later won the firm a second "E" Award.

As soon as the war ended Aeronca went back to light-plane production. The first continuous production line for private aircraft was installed, and the output increased to approximately 30 planes a day. Still manufacturing some

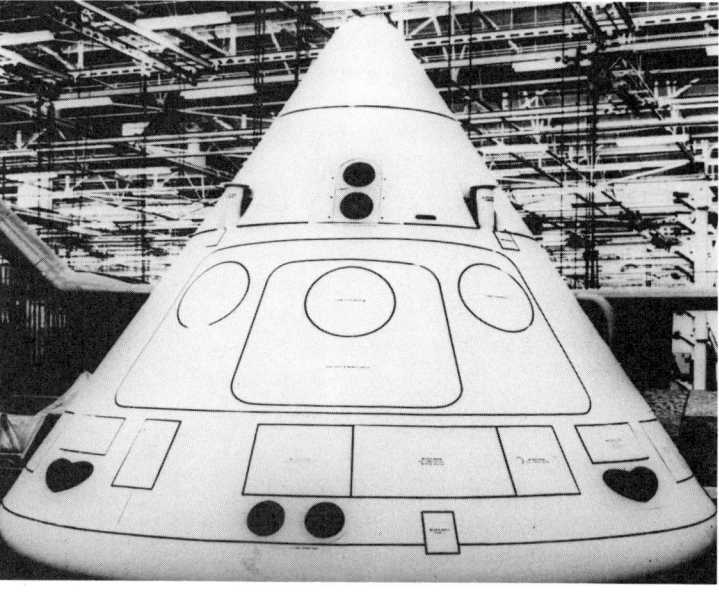

Aeronca built the outer structure of the command module for the Apollo spacecraft.

military aircraft, the company built model L-16 aircraft into 1948. The last Aeronca airplane built was delivered in 1951.

The firm had come a long way from that announcement in a 1930 *Aero Digest* of "The Most Remark-

One of the early airplanes produced by the firm was the Aeronca C-3 (shown here). The last Aeronca-built airplane was delivered in 1951.

PARTNERS IN PROGRESS

Top
An aerial view of Aeronca, Inc., 1712 Germantown Road, Middletown.

Above
Aeronca builds fairings for McDonnell Douglas' F-15 military aircraft.

able Plane in Aviation History"—the Aeronca C-2, which could develop 30 horsepower, cruise at 65 miles per hour, and weighed approximately 400 pounds.

During 1949 an orderly transition began away from the then-failing light-plane market toward a new field of subcontracting for the government and various large aircraft manufacturers. Major components for the B-47, B-52, and B-70 aircraft, maintenance stands, electronics shelters, target missiles, and varied-size parabolic reflectors were built, and in some cases designed, by Aeronca.

Aeronca has established itself as a prime producer of high-temperature brazed components used on several of the latest high-speed air and space vehicles, of bonded structures and composite assemblies, and of airframe components of a conventional form. Aeronca also designed and manufactures its own proprietary thrust reverser for executive business jets, and is also currently building shrouds for the B-1B bomber, propeller ducts for the Navy's new air-cushioned landing craft, components for Boeing 707 and 747 commercial aircraft, and components for Grumman for the F-14 and McDonnell for the F-15 military aircraft.

Aeronca, Inc., today is a leader in the engineering, development, and manufacture of major aircraft structural assemblies, jet engine components, and the manufacture of major aircraft structural assemblies.

HAMILTON INDUSTRIAL GRINDING INC.

It was the time when Dwight D. Eisenhower was President of the United States. George Bevis said to a young protégé, "Walt, if we never try, we will never know if we can make it on our own."

And so was planted the first seed of a service-oriented company specializing in the precision grinding of all types of steel. The founders decided to call the company Hamilton Industrial Grinding after the town of its birth.

By March 1961 the doors of the new business were opened. George Bevis and Walter L. Ashbrook had two machines they ran themselves. They rented space on Black Street from the Champion Paper Company—now Champion International—their first customer. Working hard, the two founders put in seven days a week, establishing themselves as a top-quality precision grinding shop.

Out of the back of his Pontiac station wagon, Walt offered pick-up and delivery service throughout the area. The company prospered and added more men and machines until it outgrew its rented quarters and had to seek larger ones. After a lengthy search a fire-damaged building was located at 240 North B Street. Formerly owned by the Hamilton Die Cast Company, the facility needed extensive reconstruction.

Working after hours and on weekends, the small company got the building ready, contracting only the work it could not complete itself. Many of the men who helped repair the structure stayed with the company. Hamilton Industrial Grinding moved into its new quarters in July 1966.

Growth continued, spurred by Hamiltonians such as Estel Stewart, Dill DeHart, and Holland "Butch" Hornung. Product line ranges from industrial cutting blades to precision machine ways. The firm's customer base runs from Mexico to California to Canada, and overseas markets include Japan.

In 1977 Hamilton Industrial Grinding Inc. opened its second plant in Asheville, North Carolina, with the main objective being to provide quality precision grinding service for the Southeast and to procure manufacturing for the mother company in Hamilton. Co-founder Walter L. Ashbrook serves as chairman of the board. His sons are also active in the firm; Walter A. Ashbrook is president and Alan John Ashbrook is vice-president.

Hamilton Industrial Grinding began operations in 1961 in this rented building on Black Street in Hamilton.

GREENWOOD CEMETERY ASSOCIATION

An act passed by the Ohio legislature on February 24, 1848, enabled, for the first time, the organization of not-for-profit cemetery associations. In Hamilton, the very next day saw John M. Millikin, John W. Erwin, and William Bebb, a past governor of Ohio who had pushed for the legislation, named as a committee to examine several locations for a new cemetery for their rapidly expanding community. A week later they brought in a report recommending the purchase of 27 acres of land northeast of Hamilton near the Miami-Erie Canal and the newly completed Hydraulic. It had, they noted, ". . . the proper subsoil, an undulating surface, a natural growth of trees, and other characteristics making it ideal for that use."

Within a month the new cemetery association was organized, lots subscribed to, trustees elected, the land purchased for $125 per acre, and the name Greenwood chosen. Other names considered were Sylvan, Hamilton, and Willow Grove.

In the fall of 1848 Millikin and Henry S. Earhart, a civil engineer and newly elected trustee, entered the grounds at the location chosen for the front gate on Heaton Street. The writer of an early account recalled that ". . . fallen leaves were lying heavy on the ground and as Millikin pushed aside leaves with his feet, Earhart, following with an armload of stakes, drove them at certain intervals. Thus were the main roads of Greenwood placed, in the depressions so the lots would occupy the higher lands." The original layout of the drives as well as 18- by 36-foot lots made in that part of the cemetery are still in use.

There was considerable public interest and approval when the cemetery was opened in March 1849, and by the end of 1850 some 250 lots had been sold for a total of $6,068.00. By 1856 the board of trustees felt so confident of the cemetery's long-term success that they purchased 16 adjacent acres from William Beckett. The transfer to Greenwood of the city-owned Soldiers' and Sailors' Fields of Honor and the purchase of additional land in 1872 and the W.H. Campbell farm in the 1930s brought the cemetery to its present total area of 96 acres.

The remains of over 1,800 previous interments were removed to Greenwood from the original Hamilton burying ground, now Fourth Ward Park, and from the Rossville burying ground, now Sutherland Park at Wayne Avenue. A poignant note is that the first burial made in the new cemetery was the infant daughter of one of the founders, Governor Bebb. Of the 6,541 burials made from 1855 to 1890, an almost unbelievable 2,622 were those of children under five years old. The total number of interments by June 1984 was 45,563.

Adolph Strauch, the well-known landscape architect and gardener who designed the nationally acclaimed Spring Grove Cemetery in Cincinnati, was frequently consulted in the further layout and planning of Greenwood. This explains why the open vistas, the extensive plantings of trees and shrubs, and the emphasis on lakes and ponds are common to both cemeteries. The prosperity of Hamilton in the late 1800s is reflected in the quality, as well as the sheer size and exuberance, of many of the markers and monuments of that era.

Since 1855 there have been only four superintendents guiding the day-to-day operations of Greenwood. They were A.J. Goshorn; Sadie Goshorn, his daughter; Paul Rogers, her nephew; and, currently, Ted Wehr. Under these superintendents and boards of trustees there has been a continuing series of improvements. Some of these are the 1884 Public Receiving Vault, a fine example of Romanesque-revival architecture now on the National Register of Historic Places; new interesting, winding drives; rare horticultural items, such as weeping mulberries and English pyramidal oaks; maintenance facilities; and impressive stone and wrought-iron entrances at Heaton Street and Greenwood Avenue. In 1948 the cemetery office was moved from its original location opposite the main gate on Heaton Street to an addition to the Campbell farmhouse. The farmhouse itself was restored and is now the superintendent's residence. A new 500-crypt garden mausoleum and chapel was dedicated on Sunday, October 25, 1983.

A 500-crypt garden mausoleum and chapel, under construction in 1983, marked the 135th year of Greenwood's participation in Hamilton's history.

THE BECKETT PAPER COMPANY

The Miami Paper Mill, a forerunner of The Beckett Paper Company.

When David Belew accepted the reins of The Beckett Paper Company in 1974, he slipped into a stream of history going back to the settling of the area in Butler County where the firm still operates. Not only is the company Hamilton's oldest operating industry; Beckett is also the oldest paper mill operating west of the Alleghenies.

The sum of $12,000 built the original mill, which began operations in 1848. In those days an enterprising young lawyer, William Beckett, who had accepted the challenge of running a paper mill from Adam Laurie, sailed into papermaking with enthusiasm and a number of different partners. In 1887 the venture became The Beckett Paper Company, incorporated under the laws of the State of Ohio.

Years of struggle followed, with the paper mill surviving because of the tenacity and courage of the family members who continued to improve and add to its facilities through good times and bad. Thomas Beckett, son of William, entered the business in 1876, at the age of 16. In 1894 Thomas introduced Buckeye Cover, the first cover paper in the industry. Buckeye Cover is still one of the 13 grades that make up Beckett's current line of fine cover and text papers.

Thomas' son, Minor, followed him as president and served until his untimely death in 1928. Guy Beckett, Thomas' nephew and grandson of the founder, joined the company that year and, after a successful career as vice-president, president, and chairman, retired in 1960. In 1933 William and Dan Beckett, also sons of Thomas, entered the business.

During the decades before World War II, Beckett had established its reputation for leadership, and by 1950 the shortage of wood pulp, along with a growing demand for Beckett papers, had resulted in the mill becoming one of the first paper companies to experience an oversold position. Much

The original Beckett Mill was constructed for $12,000 and began operations in 1848.

Beckett Paper Company's warehouse No. 2.

of that success was due to the unprecedented sales of Beckett Brilliant Opaque, introduced in 1938 as the first premium lithographic sheet in the industry.

William Beckett assumed the presidency in 1958. Under his leadership Beckett continued to research and expand its product lines, and to grow—while still located on its original site on Dayton Street. The addition of Baldwin-Lima-Hamilton buildings provided an extra 125,000 square feet of floor space.

In 1959 Beckett joined the Hammermill Paper Company organization in an exchange of shares. The purchase in late 1983 of a former Mosler Safe & Lock Company building added another 134,000 square feet of space to its holdings. The 4.6-acre site more than doubled Beckett's warehousing capacity and is designed for use in warehousing and shipping.

Throughout the firm's history its executives and other employees have contributed to the cultural, economic, spiritual, and political health of the community. Not only is the enterprise recognized as an industry leader in the field of premium printing papers, but its name has been linked with community service through the years.

Beckett papers are distributed to a worldwide market. Some of its merchants have represented the mill for more than 100 years.

The firm grew and prospered under the direction of William Beckett, grandson of the founder. Retiring in 1974, he ended a long and enduring family tradition in the paper business. Active in community affairs, he had to his credit six terms on the Hamilton City Council, two terms as mayor, and could count among his accomplishments the founding of the Miami University Pulp and Paper Foundation.

David Belew, who became president upon Beckett's retirement, has continued that legacy of community service and involvement.

An aerial view of The Beckett Paper Company mill. The firm is Hamilton's oldest operating industry.

WOODSIDE CEMETERY

Woodside Cemetery was organized on June 15, 1891, by the Woodside Cemetery Association of Middletown. Articles of incorporation were filed one week later and, as required by law, five trustees were elected to conduct business affairs. The original five members were W.H. Johnson, James Lawrence, T.A. Dickey, M.D., V.C. Hatfield, and William Caldwell.

The cemetery is located near Woodside Boulevard at 14th Avenue, adjacent to Verity Parkway on Middletown's south side. The original 100-acre tract of land, known as Winton Farm, was purchased from Dr. Dickey. A subsequent purchase of land increased the acreage to 130, with more than 50 acres not yet developed. Varieties of trees, plants, and shrubs make Woodside Cemetery one of the most beautiful facilities of its kind.

The first person to be buried in Woodside Cemetery was George Lawrence, on December 31, 1891. Since then, more than 26,000 interments have been made. Many persons prominent in the early community development have been buried in the cemetery.

In 1902 the people of Butler County built a monument to remember the soldiers and sailors who had so bravely served their country in the Army and Navy. This monument guards the military sections, where veterans of all foreign wars and the U.S. Civil War rest in plots specially designed for them. In addition, a beautiful memorial chapel was dedicated in 1951 to those individuals who had served their country during World War II.

Trustees serving in 1961, when the first mausoleum was built, included Richard Dowling, Roy O. Deardorff, L.J. Long, Harry K. Moore, Charles W. Denney, and Russell S. Weatherwax. Together, these men represent more than 140 years of service to Woodside Cemetery. Trustees continuing that tradition of service are C. Dudley Inwood, James E. Kunkler, Richard L. Lewis, William W. Raines, and Russell D. Stevens. Frederick T. Wehr serves as superintendent of the cemetery.

The beautiful memorial chapel was dedicated in 1951 to those who had served their country during World War II.

Through these entry gates lies Woodside Cemetery, which has served the people of Middletown and Butler County through 26,000 interments since 1891.

The Soldiers' and Sailors' Monument watches over the cemetery's military section, where veterans of all wars since 1902 rest.

The Soldiers, Sailors, and Pioneers Monument was dedicated in 1902. Located at the east end of the Main Street bridge in Hamilton, it is a memorial to Butler County pioneers and to all of the local veterans who served in conflicts ranging from the Indian wars through Vietnam. The displays inside include memorabilia from earliest settlement through present times. Photo by Elsie L. Bates

ADVISORY COMMITTEE

J.F. Antenen
Antenen Construction Company

C. Spencer Barkley, Administrator
Butler County Administrative Center

David L. Belew, President
Beckett Paper Company

Patrick Brown
Brown Studios

Dr. Roger Compton, Superintendent
Edgewood School District

Donald L. Dixon
Butler County Commissioner

George Estes, Superintendent
Butler County Public Schools

Patricia Hughes, Executive Director
Oxford Chamber of Commerce

James S. Irwin, Esq.
Millikin & Fitton Law Firm

Harold T. Kramer, President
Middletown Area Chamber of Commerce

Paul F. Kuhn, Superintendent
Middletown City School District

Donald C. LeRoy, Mayor
City of Fairfield

Cale L. Logsdon, President
Butler County Commissioners

Joseph L. Marcum, President
Ohio Casualty Insurance Company

Dr. Paul G. Pearson, President
Miami University

Robert Quisenberry, Superintendent
Hamilton City Schools

Dr. Larry E. Rodenberger, Superintendent
Fairfield City School District

James W. Saunders, Chairman
Middletown City Commission

Donald G. Schirmer, Vice President
Butler County Commissioners

Stephen D. Snyder, Mayor
City of Oxford

William Vollmer, President
Talawanda District
Butler County Joint Vocational School District

Robert Weigel II, Mayor
City of Hamilton

BIBLIOGRAPHY

Bartlow, Bert S.; Todhunter, W.H.; Cone, S.D.; Pater, J.J.; Schneider, F. *Centennial History of Butler County, Ohio*. Indianapolis: B.F. Bowen and Co., 1905.

Benzing, Esther R. *Census of 1807 Butler County, Ohio*. Edited by William Heiss and R.T. Mayhill. Knightstown, Ind.: Eastern Indiana Publishing Co., 1975.

Benzing, Esther R. *Fairfield Ohio—Township and City*. Mt. Healthy, Ohio: Porter Printing Co., 1978.

Blount, Jim. *The Road to Fort Hamilton*. Hamilton, Ohio: *Hamilton Journal-News*, 1976.

Butler County Atlas and Historical Review. Hamilton, Ohio: Republican Publishing Co., 1914.

Cone, S.D. *Biographical and Historical Sketches: A Narrative of Hamilton and its Residents from 1792-1896*. Hamilton, Ohio: Republican Publishing Co., 1896.

Crout, George C. *Miami Valley Vignettes*. Middletown Historical Society. Middletown, Ohio: URS Printers, 1982.

———. *Middletown Diary*. Middletown, Ohio: Private Publication, 1965. 1971. 2 vols.

———. *Middletown U.S.A.: All-America City*. Middletown, Ohio: Perry Printing Co., 1960.

Crout, George C.; Vorhis, Wilfred. *Middletown Landmarks*. Middletown, Ohio: Perry Printing Co., 1973, 1976.

Everts, L.H. *New Historical Atlas of Butler County, Ohio*. Philadelphia, Pa.: Hunter Printers, 1875.

Fall, Herbert W. *Old Middletown*. Middletown, Ohio: KGI Enterprises, 1976.

Fiftieth Anniversary Edition. Hamilton, Ohio: *Hamilton Journal-News*, Dec. 19, 1936.

Flood Souvenir Views of Hamilton, Ohio. Hamilton, Ohio: Republican Publishing Co., 1913.

Flower, Olive. *The History of Oxford College for Women 1830-1928*. Oxford, Ohio: Miami University Alumni Assoc., 1949.

Greer, Carl R. *Oxford Days*. Oxford, Ohio: Cullen Printing Co., 1947.

Havighurst, Walter; Howard, John; Gordon, Joyce, *Miami Album*. Miami University: Oxford Printing Co., 1981.

Havighurst, Walter. *The Miami Years: 1809-1959*. New York: Putnam's Sons, 1958.

Heiser, Alta Harvey. *West to Ohio*. Yellow Springs, Ohio: Antioch Press, 1954.

History and Biographical Cyclopedia of Butler County, Ohio. Cincinnati, Ohio: Western Biographical Publishing Co., 1882. (Reprinted by Butler County Historical Society.)

Howe, Henry. *Historical Collections of Ohio*. State of Ohio, Columbus. Butler County, Vol. 1, pp. 342-359, 1904.

Howells, William D. *A Boy's Town*. New York: Harper Bros, 1918. (Setting: Hamilton, Ohio.)

Huff, Thomas. *Butler County: Then and Now*. Hamilton, Ohio. 1976.

Keefe, Edward J. (ed.) *Trenton, Ohio 1816-1966*. Franklin, Ohio: Franklin Chronicle Printing Co., 1966.

Kolb, Genevieve L. and Truster, Barbara H. *Jacksonburg—Wayne Township*. Jacksonburg, Ohio: Mimeo, 1976.

Leiter, Clayton A. *Story of Butler County*. Vol. 2, pp. 424-520 in *Memoirs of the Miami Valley*. Chicago: Robert Law Co., 1919.

Looking Back—125 Years with the Middletown Journal. Middletown, Ohio. Jan. 29, 1982. Edited by Paul Day.

MacLean, J.P. *The Mound Builders: Archaeology of Butler County, Ohio*. Cincinnati, Ohio: Robert Clarke and Co., 1885.

McBride, James. *Butler County Township Maps*. 1836.

———. *Pioneer Biography*. Cincinnati, Ohio: Clarke, 1869. 2 Vols.

McClung, D.W. (ed.) *Centennial History of the City of Hamilton, Ohio*. Hamilton, Ohio: Centennial Publishing Co., 1892.

McGinnis, Ralph J. *Oxford Town*. Oxford, Ohio: Stewart Press, 1930.

Memorial Record of Butler County. Chicago: Record Publishing Co., 1894.

Middletown's 175th Birthday. *Middletown Journal*, Oct. 28, 1977. Edited by Paul Day.

Minnich, Harvey C. (ed.) *Old Favorites from the McGuffey Readers*. Cincinnati, Ohio: American Book Co., 1936.

Minnich, Harvey C. *William Holmes McGuffey Readers*. Cincinnati, Ohio: American Book Co., 1936.

Oxford Town: The Village on the Hill. Oxford, Ohio: Arthur C. Stewart Printers, 1920.

Parsons, Edward B. (ed.). *The History of the Bicentennial in Butler County*. Hamilton, Ohio: Hill Printing Co., 1977.

Schaeuble, Charlotte S. *The Geography of Hamilton*. Oxford, Ohio: Thesis, Miami University, 1948.

Shewalter, Virginia. *A History of Union Township, Butler County, Ohio*. Sharonville, Ohio: Instant Print Service, 1979.

Simms, Harry. *Middletown in Black and White*. Middletown, Ohio: Middletown Journal, 1906.

Smith, Ophia D. *Fair Oxford*. Oxford, Ohio: Oxford Historical Press, 1947.

INDEX

_____. *The Life and Times of Giles Richards.* Columbus, Ohio: Ohio Historical Society, 1937.

_____. *Oxford Spy Wed at Pistol Point.* Oxford, Ohio: Cullen Printing Co., 1962.

Smith, William E. *About the McGuffeys.* Oxford, Ohio: Cullen Printing Co., 1963.

Smith, William E.; Smith, Ophia D. *History of Southwestern Ohio: The Miami Valleys.* New York: Lewis Historical Publishing Co., 1964.

Standafer, Raymond. *History of the Miami and Erie Canal from Middletown to Cincinnati.* Oxford, Ohio: Thesis, Miami University, 1949.

Stander, Thomas F. *The Universalist Saga of Bunker Hill.* Baltimore, Md.: Gateway Press Inc., 1974.

Stroup, Hazel. *Butler County Cemetery Records.* Cincinnati, Ohio: Robert D. Craig, 1962. 6 Vols.

Taylor, Stella Weiler. *Rosemary: That's For Remembrance.* Hamilton, Ohio: Journal Publishing Co. 1940. 2 Vols. (*Index to Rosemary*, Pub. by Butler Co. Joint Vocational School, 1982.)

Upham, Alfred H. *Old Miami.* Hamilton, Ohio: Whitaker-Mohler Printing Co., 1947.

Vorhis, Wilfred D. *Methodism in Middletown, Ohio.* Dayton, Ohio: Otterbein Press, 1956. (Includes County Chronology.)

Westerhoff, John H. *McGuffey and His Readers.* Nashville, Tenn: Abington Press, 1978.

Williams, Charles W. *Minutes of Our Years: Oxford 1830-1981.* Oxford, Ohio. 1982.

Williams, Stephen R. *The Saga of Paddy's Run.* Oxford, Ohio: Miami University Alumni Association., 1972.

Partners In Progress Index
Aeronca, Inc. 114-115
Armco Inc. 108-110
Beckett Paper Company, The 118-119
Black Clawson Company 113
Butler County Historical Society 96
Community Federal Savings and Loan Association 97
First National Bank of Southwestern Ohio 100-101
Greenwood Cemetery Association 117
Hamilton Allied Corporation 99
Hamilton Caster & Mfg. Co. 98
Hamilton Industrial Grinding Inc. 116
Hamilton Tool Co., The 104
Home Federal Savings and Loan Association 111
Las-Stik Manufacturing Company, The 105
Mercy Hospital 106-107
Mosler Safe Company 102-103
Second National Bank of Hamilton 112
Woodside Cemetery 120

General Index
Italicized number indicate illustrations

A
Adrion, George *30*
Adrion, Karl *30*
Alba Manufacturing 74
All-America City Award (Middletown) 74
Allen, Joseph 36
Alston, Walter 92
Amanda 11
Amanda School 52
Appleseed, Johnny 71
Armco, Inc. 42, 66, 79, 89
Armco Park 67
Arnett, Robert 75
Arts in Middletown 63

B
Baker, John 56
Baltimore and Ohio Railroad 42
Bank of Hamilton 45
Bank One 45
Barritz, George 45
Barrows, Charles 58
Barrows, Clyde 80
Baseball Hall of Fame 92
Bates, Elsie 58
Battle of Fallen Timbers 19
Baxter, Robert *30*
Beach, Lansing 31
Bean, Douglas 91
Bebb, Edward 21
Bebb, William 21, 39, 50, 68, 79
Beckett Paper Company 45
Bein, Joseph 63
Bellew Bill 31
Benninghofen, Pauline 60
Benninghofen House *82*
Benzing, Esther 74
Bering Strait 12
Bethany Station 90
Betsey Newton Memorial Arboretum 71
Bienville, Celeron de *10*
Bijou Opera House 65
Bishop, Robert H. 49
Black, Johnny 91
Blount, James 39, 56
Blue Jacket (Marmaduke Van Swearingen) 22
Blust's Castle *76*
Boryca, Pat *85*
Boxwell, Alexander 52
Boy's Town, A (book) 57
Brady, James 25
Brown, Henry 25
Brown, Patrick 58
Buffalo Creek 15
Bull's Run Arboretum 71
Burnet, Jacob 25
Butler, Richard 15, 18, 19
Butler Bowl 66
Butler County Board of Education 55
Butler County Court House *88*, 92, *93*
Butler County Democrat (newspaper) 55
Butler County Fair 36, *37*, 66
Butler County Historical Society 60
Butler County Industrial Development Department 89
Butler County Musical Association 63
Butler County Private Industry Council 89
Butler County Sports Hall of Fame 92
Butler Tavern 52
Butts, Robert *30*

C
Cahill, Harry *30*
Campbell, Robert 27
Campbell, James 79
Campbell, Lewis 39, 55
Canal Bank 45
Canal Museum 47, 61
Carnegie, Andrew 90
Centinel of the Northwestern Territory (newspaper) 55
Central High School 77
Chamberlin, Caroline A. 56
Champion Coated Paper Mill 45
Champion International Corp. 68
Chesapeake and Ohio Railroad 42
Chicago 34, 40
Christy, Andrew 25
Churches and Religious Institutions 49, 50
Cincinnati 27, 31, 34, 42, 45, 50, 63, 77, 79
Cincinnati, Dayton, and Toledo Traction Company 31

INDEX

Cincinnati, Hamilton, and Dayton Railroad 40, 42, *43*, 46
Cincinnati and Springfield Railway Company 42
Citizens Bank 45
Civil War 36, 42, 58, 74
Civilian Conservation Corps 80
Clark, George Rogers 15
Clark, James 56
Cleveland, Columbus, Cincinnati, and Indianapolis Railroad 42
Clevenger, Shobal Vail 58
Clinton, DeWitt 27
Clokey, Joseph 63
Club Dardanella 91
Colonial Theater 65
Columbia 39
Conrail 42
Corn 34, 35
Cox, James 79, *79*
Craig, Henry *30*
Craig, Paul *30*
Crawford House 68
Cummins, George 58
Custer, George 19

D
Darke, William 18
Davis, Benjamin 25
Day, Doris (Doris Von Kappelhoff) 91
Denman, Matthias 17
Dennison, William 50
Detroit 34
Diebold, Inc. 42
Diehl, Bruce 71
Dixon's Opera House 63
Do You Know How It Feels? (book) 56
Doty, Daniel 21, 25, 27, 39
Doty, L.D. 45
Doty's Grove *26*, 67
Dunbar, Paul Laurence 57
Dunn, James 23

E
Earhart, Henry 39
Eaton Manor Restaurant 91
Ellis, S.H. 36
Enoch, Abner 25, 27
Erie Canal 27
Erwin, John 35, 39
Essman, Mary Pat 91
Eugene H. Hughes Memorial Tuberculosis and Mental Hospital 60
Ewbank, Weeb 92
Excello 11, 68

F
Fairfield 21, 73, 74
Fairfield Civic Association 74
Fall, Herbert 58, *58*
Farmer's College 56
Fenwick, Edward 50
Finkelman, Harry 65

First Marine Band 86
First National Bank of Middletown 45
Fitton, Samuel 45, 46
Fort Ancient 14
Fort Finney 15
Fort Hamilton 18, 19, *21*, 50
Fort Hamilton Hospital 60
Fort Jefferson 19
Fort Recovery 18
Fort Washington *18*
Furman, Nathaniel 52
Furman Institute 52

G
Gallagher, John 55
Gard, Homer 55
Gard, Stephen 49
Gear, Jean 56
German Village 72
Globe Opera House 63
Goldflies, Bruce 58
Goldflies, Eugene 63
Goodman, Samuel 46
Goudi, John 31
Goulder, Grace 73
Governor Brown (canalboat) 28
Governor Bebb Park 68
Great Butler Mound 12, *13*
Great Depression 46, 80
Great Flood of 1913 77, 79
Great Miami River *10*, 11, 12, 14, 15, 17, 18, 23, 27, 33, 34, 35, 39, 65, 66, 77
Greater Hamilton Chamber of Commerce 89
Green, John 25
Greer, John 23
Grimes, James 50

H
Halstead, John 21
Halstead, Murat 21, 50, 56
Hamilton, Alexander 18
Hamilton, Irvin 63
Hamilton and Eaton Railroad 42
Hamilton and Rossville Hydraulic Company 39, 40
Hamilton Club 31
Hamilton Daily Democrat (newspaper) 55
Hamilton Dime Savings Bank 45
Hamilton Evening Journal (newspaper) 55
Hamilton First National Bank 45
Hamilton Journal-News (newspaper) 55, 92
Hamilton Municipal Band 63
Hamilton River 11
Hamilton Street Railway and Electric Company 89
Hamilton Symphony Orchestra 63
Hamilton Telegraph (newspaper) 55
Hammerstein, Oscar 91
Hancock, John 21

Harbaum, Will *70*
Harding-Jones Paper Company 68
Harmar, Josiah 17, 18
Harris, Andrew 79
Harris, Bambo 39
Harrison, William Henry 27
Havighurst, Marion Boyd 57
Havighurst, Walter 57
Helsel, Dale 74
Heming-Hall Safe Company 42
Hickory Flats 12
Hindman, John 15
History of Southwestern Ohio (book) 57
Hoffman, Ben 31
Hollenbaugh, Alice 75
Homestead Act 36
Hook, George 77
Howard, John 75
Howells, William Dean 50, 56, 57
Hoxie, George 58
Hubbert, William 25
Hueston Woods State Park 60, 71
Huff, Thomas 75
Hughes, Micajah 45
Hughes School *50*
Hurst, Fannie 91, 92

I
Ice Age 12
Ice making *30*
Illinoian Glacier 11
Indian Creek Church 87
Indian Creek Park 68
Indianapolis 42

J
Jefferson, Thomas 25
Jewell Theatre *64*
Johns, Marie 67
Johnson, W.H. 31
Jones, Clarence *30*
Jones, Thomas *30*
Junction Railroad Company 42

K
Kansas Glacier 11
Keefe, Edward 75
Kelley, Edgar Stillman 63
Kelley, Oliver H. 36
Kessler, Patrick 75, *75*, 77
KIO League 67
Kit Curry 66
Kitchel, John 23
Kobler, John 49
Kramer, Harold 58
Krider, Edward 36
Kyger, H.D. 66

L
Lady Hamilton (canalboat) 31
Lady Pugh 35
Lake Erie and Miami Packet Company 31

125

Landis, Kenesaw Mountain 67, 92
Lane, Clark 40, 90
Lane-Hooven House *84*
Lane Public Library 58, 90, *90*
LaTourrette, P.P. 40
Lecklider, Ben 46
Lee, Dale Russell 52
Lewis Place *84*
Liberty Township Historical Society 61
Littell's Living Age (magazine) 56
Little Bighorn 19
Little Miami River 17
Little Prairie Baptist Church 39
Little Turtle 14, 18
Lucas, Jerry 92
Ludlow, Israel 23, 25

M
Magaw, Samuel 49
Magie, David 33
Magie Farm *85*
Magie hogs 33
Maple Knoll Hospital and Home 60
Martin, John 27
McBride, James 55, 57
McClellan, Lula 91
McClellan, Robert 91
McClelland, William 25
McCormick Reaper 40
McCullough, Samuel 21
McCullough-Hyde Hospital 60
McGonigle 21
McGuffey, William Holmes 49, 55, 60
McGuffey Readers 49, 55
McKinley, William 79
McLaughlin, Ebenezer *30*
McLaughlin, P.J. *30*
McLaughlin, Richard *30*
McMechan, Jane 56
Mercy Hospital 58, 60
Miami Canal 12, 27, 28, *29*, 31, 34, 35, 40, 61, 67, 80
Miami Canal Park 68
Miami College 36
Miami Conservancy District 79
Miami Field 66, 92
Miami Indians *13*, 14
Miami Intelligencer (newspaper) 55
Miami Paper Mill *38*
Miami River Park 68
Miami University 45, 49, *54*, 55, 56, 57, 58, 60, 63, 66, 67, 68, 74, *83*, 92
Miami Valley National Bank 45
Middfest *86*
Middletown 2, 11, 14, 17, 23, 25, 27, 31, 34, 39, 40, 45, 49, 52, 66, 73, 79
Middletown Area Chamber of Commerce 89
Middletown Historical Society 61
Middletown Hospital *59*, 60
Middletown Journal (newspaper) 92
Middletown Library 91, *91*
Middletown Mail (newspaper) 56

Middletown Symphony Orchestra 63
Miller Brewing Company 75
Mills, James 56
Miltonville 39
Minnich, Harvey 60
Moeller, Bill 92
Monfort, Francis 49
Monroe, James 21
Monroe Historical Society 61
Moon, Lottie 56, *74*, 75
Morgan, Arthur 79
Morgan, John 66
Morrell, Calvin 25
Morrow, Jeremiah 27
Morton, John 63
Mosler Safe Company 42, *43*
Mosopelea 14
Mound Builders 12
Murray, Bonnie 91
Music Hall 63

N
Nardiello, Jerry 92
National Currency Act 45
National Farm Organization 37
National Grange 36, 37, 52
National Municipal League 74
New Orleans 34
New York Central Railroad 42
Nuxhull, Joe 92, *92*

O
Oglesby, Robert 75
Oglesby, William 45
Ohio Casualty 46
Ohio Hall of Fame 42
Ohio Historical Society 42
Ohio River 15, 49
Ohio State Association of Photographers 58
Orcut, Darius 25
Ordinance of 1787 55
Osborn, Henry 74
Osbourn, Cyrus 25
Overpeck, Lucien 58
Oxford 21, 49, 55, 66, 73, 74
Oxfrd Museum Association 60
Oxford Press 56
Oxford Town Square 67

P
Page, Doris 67
Palace Theater 65
Parker, Bonnie 80
Parseghian, Ara 92
Parsons, S.H. 15
Pater Park 68
Pearce, Michael 49
Penn-Central Railroad 42
Pennsylvania Railroad 42
Perry, Dick 74
Pickawillany 14
Pioneer Farm and House Museum 60

Pioneer Village 68, *69*
Piqua 15
Playmates of the Towpath (book) 31
Poland-China hog 33, 34
Polar Bear Tobacco *41*
Pork 32, 33, 34, *35*
Potter, Enow 25
Potter, Moses 25
Prohibition 79
Purcell, John 50

R
Radio and Television Stations 90
Randolph, Benjamin 25
Rathman's Drug Store *59*
Reily, John 23, 25
Rentschler Forest Preserve *70*
Rentschler Park 68
Review of Reviews (magazine) 56
Rialto Theater 65
Richmond and Miami Railroad 42
Ritchie, John 50
Robinson, Joseph 15
Roosevelt, Franklin 79, 80
Roosevelt, Theodore 75
Root, Charley 92
Rossville 23, 25
Rossville Female Academy 52
Ruffin, William 25

S
Samuel Forrer (canalboat) 27, 28
Scripps, E.W. 52
Sebald Park 68
Second National Bank of Hamilton 45
Sept, John 15
Shartle, Charles 45
Shaw, Albert 56
Shawnee Indians 14
Sheard, Kim *69*
Silvers, James 23
Simmons, John 15
Simon, Frank 91, *92*
Skinner, John 39
Sloneker, Howard 46
Smith, James 25
Smith, Ophia 57
Smith, William *54*, 57
Smith Library of Regional History 90
Sohngen, Charles 46
Sorg, Paul 45, 65, 79
Sorg Mansion *83*
Sorg Opera House *62*, *64*, 65
Sorg Paper Company 40
Sorg Tobacco Company 65
Sousa, John Philip 91
Southern Ohio Traction Company 89
Soybeans 35
Spanish-American War 75
Square D Company 74
St. Clair, Arthur 18, 19, *20*
St. Clair Recreational Area 71
St. John, Lynn 92

INDEX

Stander, Thomas 75
Stites, Benjamin 17, 23
Storer, E.T. 56
Sulzer-Escher-Wyss, Inc. 40
Sunset Park 43
Sutherland, John 25
Sutphin, Jane Potter *24*
Sutphin, John 27, 45
Sutton, David 23
Sutton, James 25
Sycamore Grove 67
Sycamore Grove Academy 50
Symmes, John Cleves 17, *20*
Symmes Purchase 17

T
Teays 11
Temple, Charles 63
They Made the News (book) 56
Thomas, Jill *69*
Thomson, Peter 45
Thomson Park 67
Tobias, Anthony 40
Todhunter, Louise 91
Torrence, John 25
Torrence, Ridgely 56
Treaty of Fort Finney 15
Treaty of Greenville 19
Trenton 11, 21, 73, 75
Trenton Historical Society 61
Trenton Sesquicentennial 61
Tytus, John 42

U
Union Mutual Insurance Company 46

V
Vail, Hugh 27
Vail, Stephen 21, 23, 25, 39
Vanderveer, Peter 27
Vanness, Garrett 25
Verity, George Matthew 42, *42*, 66
Voice of America (radio) 90

W
Wade, Elisha 25
Walker, Paul 92
Wallace, Matthew 50
Warren County Museum 61
Washington, George 15, 17
Watts, Richard 25
Wayne, Anthony 18, 19, *20*
Weatherwax Golf Course 66
Webster, Taylor 55
Webster, William 45
West, William 15
Western College *48*, 55, 63, 66
Wheat 34, 35
White, George 58
White, Robert 56
Wiles, Isaac 25
Wilkinson, Valda 63
Wisconsin Glacier 11

Woodmansee, James 56
Woods, John 55
World War I 75
World War II 67, 74

Y
Yager Stadium 92
Yeatman's Cove 17

THIS BOOK WAS SET IN
PALATINO AND PONTIAC TYPES,
PRINTED ON
70-POUND BECKETT CAMBRIC COLONIAL WHITE,
COLOR SECTION PRINTED ON 70-POUND CHAMPION JAVELIN,
AND BOUND BY
WALSWORTH PUBLISHING COMPANY